Contents

Lesson	Topic/Vocabulary	Language	Page
Welcome: A great adventure!	*detective, missing*		4
1 Where's Toto?	*clever, niece, nephew, friendly, helpful*	Present simple	6
2 We're getting ready!	*laptop, binoculars, compass, can opener, need, diary, torch*	Present continuous	8
3 Dr Wild drives well.	*well, carefully, badly, slowly, quietly, happily, quickly*	Adverbs of manner	10
4 Skills: Let's phone Mel.		Functional language: saying your phone number Writing Class: punctuation	12
FlyHigh File: Countries and nationalities	*country, capital city, flag, nationality, language*	Present simple; present continuous	14
5 There was a storm.	*storm, behind, windy, thunder and lightning, in front of*	*There was/were/wasn't/weren't*	16
6 We landed on a beach.	*aquarium, town hall, police station, pet shop, museum, café*	Past simple regular: affirmative	18
7 Did you talk to them?	*notice, blond, moustache, beard, thin, wavy, face*	Past simple regular: negatives and questions	20
8 Skills: I'd like tickets for the museum, please.		Functional language: asking for tickets Writing Class: *and* and *but*	22
FlyHigh File: Hurricanes	*hurricane, last, flood, cause, tornado, produce, travel, destroy, natural disaster*	Present simple; past simple	24
The **FlyHigh** Review 1			26
Storytime: Robinson Crusoe	*ill, tool, gun, knife, journey, land, island, tent, cave, strange, footprint*		28
9 Magnus and Claudia had an accident!	*farm, cow, grass, owl, pond, bull*	Past simple irregular: affirmative	30
10 Did they find Toto?	*scared, confused, nervous, unhappy*	Past simple irregular: negatives and questions	32
11 Claudia couldn't hear.	*well, cold, headache, sore throat, earache, ill stomachache*	*could/couldn't*	34
12 Skills: I'm sorry I couldn't come.		Functional language: giving reasons and describing what you have done Writing Class: *on, in, at* with days and times	36
FlyHigh File: Dinosaurs	*continent, plant, lizard, land, sea, sky*	Past simple; *could/couldn't*	38
13 They went through the town.	*train station, road, market, castle, bridge*	Prepositions of movement: *along, past, across, around, through*	40
14 How much were the tickets?	*money, seat, search, carriage, look after, luggage*	Quantifiers: *much, many, a lot of, a little, a few*	42
15 I heard something!	*stew, rice, cabbage, steak, peas*	*somebody/anybody/nobody/something/anything/nothing*	44
16 Skills: I'd like chips.		Functional language: saying what you would like to eat and drink Writing Class: *first, then, afterwards, finally*	46
FlyHigh File: London bus tour	*art gallery, cathedral, church, tower, Big Wheel, bell, bridge, hill, street*	Past simple	48
The **FlyHigh** Review 2			50
Storytime: Alice in Wonderland	*hare, place, wine, tea, polite, wide, angrily*		52
17 Is it yours?	*rescue, scarf, glove, jacket, belt, trainers, tie*	Possessive pronouns	54
18 You don't have to shout!	*arrive, leave, start, lose, bring, finish*	*have to/don't have to* *has to/doesn't have to*	56
19 Dr Wild went to the bank to get some money.	*bank, post office, send, find, garage, hire*	Infinitives of purpose	58
20 Skills: I arrive at twenty to nine.		Functional language: saying the time Writing Class: writing the time	60

Lesson	Topic/Vocabulary	Language	Page
FlyHigh File: Clothes through the ages	Ordinal numbers: *11th* to *21st* *breeches, cap, trainers, tunic, apron*	Past simple	62
21 The red van is faster!	*van, motorbike, fire engine, scooter, helicopter*	Comparatives with *-er*	64
22 They are the silliest people in the world!	*silly, catch, runner, noisy, light*	Superlatives with *-est*	66
23 Oscar's got the most comfortable bed!	*expensive, soft, comfortable, modern, dangerous, exciting, tobogganing*	Comparatives and superlatives with *more* and the *most*	68
24 Skills: Which bike do you like best?	*wheel, gears, handle bars, brake, saddle*	Functional language: comparing different items Writing Class: adjective order	70
FlyHigh File: Planets	*planet, rock, ring, gas, star, ice, furthest*	Present simple; comparatives and superlatives	72
The **FlyHigh** Review 3			74
Storytime: The Prince and the Pauper	*palace, poor, beg, gates, soldiers, beggar, rich, servant, cheap, pauper*		76
25 I want to join in.	*join in, fancy dress, costume, alien, superhero, pop star*	*want to* + infinitive	78
26 He likes tobogganing!	*ice skating, surfing, skateboarding, rock climbing, cycling, fishing*	*like* + *-ing* *be good at* + *-ing* *I'm happy when I'm … ing*	80
27 What shall we do?	*use, escape, reach, borrow, hold*	*Shall we …?* *What about … ing?*	82
28 Skills: Shall we meet in the park or at my house?		Functional language: making arrangements Writing Class: using *or* in questions	84
FlyHigh File: Sporting legends	*football player, goal, score, world record, Olympic flag, gold medal, medicine, compete, train*	Present simple; past simple; comparatives and superlatives	86
29 I'm going to phone the police!	*knock over, lamp, curtain, rug, sofa, cushion, prison*	Future: affirmative with *going to*	88
30 Are they going to come home now?	*plan, picnic, invitation, banner*	Future: negatives and question with *going to*	90
31 Why did they want Toto?	*rare, robber, steal, jewellery, valuable, painting, diamond*	*Why? Because*	92
32 Skills: Would you like to come to our party?		Functional language: inviting someone to a party Writing Class: writing dates	94
FlyHigh File: Duke of Edinburgh's Award	*award, physical, volunteering, skills, expedition, photography, sewing, knitting, DJ*		96
The **FlyHigh** Review 4			98
Storytime: The Voyages of Sindbad the Sailor	*sailor, voyage, dangerous, captain, ship, sail, wood, afraid*		100
33 Jack has disappeared!	*disappear, explain, return, hot air balloon, trip*	Present perfect: affirmative (recent events)	102
34 Have you seen these photos?	*horse riding, camping, canoeing, Chinese, restaurant*	Present perfect: negatives and questions (life experiences)	104
35 I haven't brushed Oscar yet!	*brush, polish, change*	Present perfect with *yet*	106
36 Skills: You should take your camera.		Functional language: giving advice with *should/shouldn't* Writing Class: writing an address	108
FlyHigh File: The Arctic and Antarctic	*North Pole, South Pole, Arctic, Antarctic, scientist, light, dark, polar bear, walrus, seal, fox, whale, penguin*	Present simple; comparatives and superlatives	110
Goodbye: Party time!			112
The **FlyHigh** Review 5			114
The **FlyHigh** Show: The amazing adventure!			116
Teacher's Day	*Ancient Greece, wax, stick, wrestling, strict, hit*		118
Valentine's Day	*message, rose, violet, heart*		120
The Queen's Birthday	*gun salute, garden, midday, parade*		122
Word List			124
Irregular Verbs			126

Welcome

A great adventure!

① Hello, Jack. Hello, Kelly.

Hello, Aunt Sophie!

Hi, Oscar!

② Who are they?

They're our friends at school.

Mel, Beth, Harry and Kit.

① **Match.**

1 Dr Wild / Aunt Sophie   2 Jack   3 Kelly   4 Oscar

 a

 b

 c

 d

Our Aunt Sophie's really cool
We stay with her when we haven't got school.
She's Dr Wild, Animal Detective!
Dr Wild, Animal Detective!
She can find your animals for you!
Is an animal missing from the zoo?
Ask Dr Wild. She can help you!
She's Dr Wild, Animal Detective!
Dr Wild, Animal Detective!
She can find your animals for you!

③ **Read and write True or False.**

1 Jack and Kelly are brother and sister. ___True___

2 Dr Wild is their aunt. _____

3 Oscar is their friend from school. _____

4 Mel, Harry, Kit and Beth are their friends from school. _____

5 Dr Wild is a teacher. _____

6 Dr Wild can find missing animals. _____

5

Where's Toto?

1 Dr Wild, Animal Detective!

Hello, it's Sally here. I can't find Toto the toucan. He isn't in the zoo! Can you help me?

DR WILD ANIMAL DETECTIVE

2 Yes, of course. What does Toto look like?

He's black and white. He's funny and clever. He likes bananas.

3 My niece Kelly and my nephew Jack are with me. And my cat Oscar, of course!

DR WILD ANIMAL DETECTIVE

4 Oscar?

Yes, he's lazy but he's very friendly. We can all help.

Thank you. You're very helpful.

5 Does Sally work at the zoo, Aunt Sophie?

Yes, she does.

What does she do?

She's a keeper. She's very kind. She loves animals.

6 Do you know where Toto is?

No, I don't. I don't know where Toto is.

MISSING!

NAME: TOTO
COLOUR: BLACK AND WHITE
HOBBIES: EATING BANANAS

Learn with Oscar

I/You/We/They
I live with Dr Wild.
We don't live at the zoo.
Do Kelly and Jack live with you?
No, they don't.

He/She/It
Dr Wild works at home.
She doesn't work at the zoo.
Does she like animals?
Yes, she does.

① Read the story and answer.

1 Is Toto in the zoo? ..... No, he isn't. .....
2 What does Toto look like? ....
3 Who are Kelly and Jack? ....

4 Is Toto lazy? ....
5 Where does Sally work? ....
6 Does Dr Wild know where Toto is? ....

② Listen and tick.

	lazy	helpful	kind	funny	clever
		✔			

③ Complete the questions. Then ask and answer.

What   How   are   is   live   are   ~~What's~~

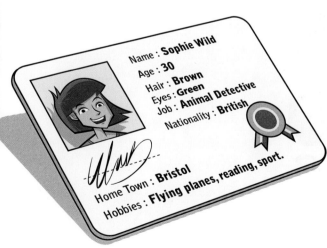

Name : **Sophie Wild**
Age : **30**
Hair : **Brown**
Eyes : **Green**
Job : **Animal Detective**
Nationality : **British**
Home Town : **Bristol**
Hobbies : **Flying planes, reading, sport.**

1 ..... What's ..... her name? Her name is ..... Sophie Wild ..... .
2 .... old is she? She's ....
3 What colour .... her hair? It's ....
4 What colour .... her eyes? They're ....
5 What's her job? She's an ....
6 .... nationality is she? She's ....
7 Where does she .... ? She ....
8 What .... her hobbies?
Her hobbies are ....

2

 laptop   binoculars   compass   can opener   need   diary   torch

We're getting ready!

Harry: Mel, Beth, Kit, come and see! Jack, Kelly and Dr Wild are talking on the video on my laptop. Hi, Jack! Hi, Kelly! What are you doing?

Jack: Hi, Harry. We're getting ready.

Harry: Are you packing your bags?

Jack: Yes, we are. We're going to find Toto the toucan.

Harry: What are you taking?

Jack: I'm taking binoculars, a compass and a can opener!

Harry: Great!

Jack: We need a torch!

Kelly: I've got one! I'm taking my diary too.

Dr Wild: I've got my laptop and our passports. That's it. We're ready.

Kelly: Come on, Oscar. We're leaving!

① **Read and write.**

1 Jack has got binoculars .

2 ....

3 ....

4 ....

5 ....

6 ....

7 ....

8

I/You/We/They

What are you doing?
Are you sleeping, Oscar?
No, I'm not. I'm watching Jack and Kelly.
What are they doing? They're packing their bags.

He/She/It

He's taking a can opener.
She's taking my food.

② **Look, ask and answer.**

wearing   eating   drinking   doing homework   talking   reading   listening   writing

Mel
Harry
Beth
Kit

Is Beth eating an apple?

No, she isn't.
She's eating a sandwich.

What's she wearing?

She's wearing a pink T-shirt.

③ **Choose and write.**

torch   ~~compass~~   binoculars   diary   can opener   laptop

1 Where am I? Where do I go now?
I need a ___compass___ .

2 He's sending an email on his _____ .

3 I'm watching birds with my _____ .

4 It's dark. I can't see! I need a _____ .

5 I write in my _____ every day.

6 I can't open this can of fish.
I need a _____ .

④ **Listen, choose and write. Then sing.**

find   ~~looking~~   black   is   know   want   don't   isn't   called

We're (1) ___looking___ for a bird called Toto.
We don't (2) _____ where he is.
He (3) _____ in the zoo,
We (4) _____ know where to go.
We (5) _____ to find him!

We're looking for a bird (6) _____ Toto.
We don't know where he (7) _____ .
He's (8) _____ and white,
We hope he's all right.
We want to (9) _____ him!

3

well

carefully

badly

slowly

quietly

happily

quickly

Dr Wild drives well.

Dr Wild drives carefully. She doesn't drive badly. She drives well.

Kelly sees a feather in the road!

Dr Wild stops the car slowly.

They look at the feather.

'I think this is Toto's feather,' says Jack quietly.

'Yes!' says Kelly happily. She can see two more feathers.

'I need the binoculars please, Jack,' says Dr Wild.

She can see a man and a woman in a small boat.

'I think that is Claudia Fox and Magnus Wolf. They're very bad people!

We need a boat!' she says. 'Come on! Quickly!'

Learn with Oscar

Dr Wild drives carefully.
Oscar sleeps quietly.

careful	carefully
happy	happily
good	well

① **Read the story and write True or False.**

1 Dr Wild drives carefully and well. _True_
2 She stops the car quickly. _____
3 They can see Toto's feathers. _____

4 Kelly can see Toto. _____
5 Dr Wild likes Claudia and Magnus. _____

② **Match and write.**

~~badly~~   slowly   well   quickly   happily   quietly

1 _e_ He's drawing _badly_ .
2 _____ She's singing _____ .
3 _____ They're walking _____ .

4 _____ She's running _____ .
5 _____ They're playing _____ .
6 _____ He's sleeping _____ .

③ **Think and write with Dr Wild.**

drive   talk   eat   run   sing   draw   write   read

Think about you, your friends and your family. How do they do these things?

My friend Pauline talks quickly.
_____
_____
_____
_____
_____
_____
_____

4 Let's phone Mel.

SKILLS

(1) Look at the photo. Then read and circle.

All about me

My name is Mel Taylor. I live in Bristol, in England. I'm tall and I've got **(1)** short / long **(2)** brown / red hair and **(3)** brown / green eyes. I've got a small family, my mum, my dad, my **(4)** sister / brother and me. I love talking to my friends on the phone. I'm friendly and I think I'm helpful too. I usually help my mum and dad in the house at the weekends and then go out with my friends. I like playing on the computer, **(5)** reading / drawing and **(6)** playing volleyball / swimming. I'm good at **(7)** volleyball / swimming and I swim **(8)** slowly / quickly and **(9)** well / badly.

(2) Read and answer.

1 Where does Mel live? _In Bristol_ .

2 What are her hobbies? ....

3 What does she do at the weekends? ....

4 Is she lazy? ....

Writing Class: punctuation

(3) Look at these examples.

Then look at Mel's homework again.
Count the punctuation.

Has Mel's brother got a bike, a watch and rollerblades?
Yes, he has.

1 CAPITAL LETTERS _18_ ....

2 Apostrophes ['] ....

3 Commas [,] ....

4 Question marks [?] ....

5 Full stops [.] ....

4 Listen and write the numbers. Then ask your friends and write.

⊕ name .....Mel.......... ❯
⊕ number .6754430...... ❯

⊕ name .....Beth......... ❯
⊕ number .... ❯

⊕ name .....Harry........ ❯
⊕ number .... ❯

⊕ name .....Kit.......... ❯
⊕ number .... ❯

What's your phone number?

It's ...

⊕ name .... ❯
⊕ number .... ❯

⊕ name .... ❯
⊕ number .... ❯

⊕ name .... ❯
⊕ number .... ❯

⊕ name .... ❯
⊕ number .... ❯

5 Listen and circle.

1 Where's Kit?

2 What's he doing?

3 What does he want to do later?

4 Where's Mel?

5 What's she doing?

6 What does she want to do later?

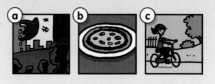

6 Choose places from 5 and write. Then act it out.

Hi, ...

Where are you?

What are you doing?

Do you want to .... later?

Bye.

Hello!

I'm ....

I'm ....

....   Bye.

FlyHigh File: Countries and nationalities

1 **Read about the United Kingdom.**

FACTFILE

Country: The United Kingdom
Capital City: London
Nationality: British
Language: English

Heathrow is a very big airport in London. London is the capital city of the United Kingdom. Aeroplanes fly to lots of different countries from Heathrow every day.

What do you need when you travel by plane? You need a passport and a ticket. Look at these children. They're travelling to their home countries. Where do you think they come from?

2 **Look and guess. Where do the children come from?**

Russia	England	the USA	Argentina	France
Turkey	Ukraine	Poland	Spain	Australia

3 Read and check. Then number.

[ ] My name is Marina and I'm Argentinian. I'm travelling to Argentina. I live in the capital city, Buenos Aires. Buenos Aires is a beautiful city! I speak Spanish. My flag is blue and white.

[1] I'm Russian and my name is Anton. Russia is a very big country! I live in the capital city, Moscow. I speak Russian. My flag is white, red and blue.

[ ] I'm Marko, I'm Ukrainian and I'm travelling to Ukraine. I live in the capital city, Kiev. There are lots of great places to go in Kiev. I speak Ukrainian and my flag is blue and yellow.

[ ] I'm Agata and I'm going to my country, Poland. I live in the capital city, Warsaw. I speak Polish. My flag is white and red. I'm Polish. I love my country!

4 Read and complete.

FACT FILE

Country:
Argentina

Capital City:

Nationality:

Language:

FACT FILE

Country:

Capital City:
Moscow

Nationality:

Language:

FACT FILE

Country:

Capital City:

Nationality:
Polish

Language:

FACT FILE

Country:

Capital City:

Nationality:

Language:
Ukrainian

My Project

Make a passport.

Name
Arda Berkan

City
Ankara

Nationality
Turkish

Language
Turkish

I'm Arda and I'm from Turkey. I live in Ankara. I speak Turkish. My flag is red and white. I'm Turkish.

15

5

 storm

 behind

 windy

 thunder and lightning

 in front of

There was a storm.

①

Yesterday evening we were on a small boat. Our boat was behind Claudia and Magnus's boat.

We were near Toto but Dr Wild was worried. There were big black clouds in the sky. Suddenly there was heavy rain and it was very windy. There was a terrible storm with thunder and lightning.

It was a bad night on the boat.

②

In the morning it was sunny and we were safe but there weren't any boats near us. Claudia and Magnus's boat wasn't in front of us.

We were near a beach and there was a town not far away. But where were Claudia and Magnus?

Where was Toto? Were they in the town?

There was a storm.
Was there a town?

There wasn't a boat in front of them.

There were black clouds.
Were there any people?

There weren't any boats behind them.

---

① Read the story and write True or False.

1 Dr Wild was on a big boat. ..False..

2 Jack was worried. ....

3 It was windy and there was a storm in the night. ....

4 There was thunder and lightning in the morning. ....

5 There weren't any boats behind them in the morning. ....

6 There was a town near the beach. ....

---

② Listen and number. Then ask and answer.

| ① Poland | ② Argentina | ③ Russia | ④ Ukraine | ⑤ England | ⑥ Turkey |

1

What was the weather like in Poland yesterday?

It was snowy.

---

③ Write There was/were or There wasn't/weren't.

1 ...There were... two big boats on the sea.

2 .... one small boat.

3 .... two children with their mum.

4 .... any sand on the beach.

5 .... any clouds in the sky.

We were here last summer.

 aquarium
 town hall
 police station
 pet shop
 museum
 café

We landed on a beach.

We've got an email from Jack and Kelly.

Can you read it, Harry?

To: Harry@flyhigh.com, Beth@flyhigh.com

From: Jack@flyhigh.com

Subject: We landed on a beach!

Hello,

How are you? We're having an exciting trip.

Yesterday we landed on a beach in France. Then we walked to a town. It wasn't far. We looked for Toto all morning. He wasn't in the park. He wasn't in the zoo but Oscar liked the aquarium. We asked about Toto in the town hall and the police station. We looked in the pet shop. There were some pretty yellow birds and a noisy parrot but Toto wasn't there. In the afternoon we visited the library, the museum and a café! The café makes delicious cakes!

We are very worried. We can't find Toto.

Email us soon.

Kelly and Jack

① Read and match.

1 Jack and Kelly are in	**a** the zoo.
2 There was an aquarium in	**b** the café.
3 There were some yellow birds in	**c** Toto.
4 There were some delicious cakes in	**d** the pet shop.
5 Jack and Kelly can't find	**e** a town in France.

Learn with Oscar

Yesterday we landed on a beach.   We walked to a town.
We looked for Toto.

2 **Listen and circle. Then say.**

1 ask for help /
(a map)

2 look at the dinosaurs
/ the watches

3 wait for a friend
/ a table

Yesterday, Magnus
asked for a map.

4 watch the fish
/ the sharks

5 play with a rabbit
/ a dog

6 listen to a talk about birds
/ a concert

3 **Look at 2 and write.**

1 He ...asked for a map... in the police station.
2 They .... in the museum.
3 She .... in the café.

4 They .... in the aquarium.
5 She .... in the pet shop.
6 They .... in the town hall.

4 **Listen and number the pictures. Then sing.**

1
Yesterday I stayed at home.
Yesterday I helped my dad.
Yesterday I washed the car,
Yesterday morning.

2
Yesterday I walked to the park.
Yesterday I played with my friends.
Yesterday I jumped and skipped,
Yesterday afternoon.

3
Yesterday I watched TV.
Yesterday I listened to music.
Yesterday I looked at the stars,
Yesterday evening.

notice	blond	moustache	beard	thin	wavy	face

Did you talk to them?

Kelly and Jack didn't find Toto yesterday. They decided to ask for help.

Excuse me. We're looking for this bird. Can you help us?

Yes, I can.

2 This morning a car stopped here. There was a toucan in the car.

3 Did you notice a man and a woman in the car?

Yes, I did.

What did the man look like?

4 He was short with a blond moustache and beard.

5 And the woman?

The woman was tall and thin with wavy hair. I didn't look at her face.

It was Magnus and Claudia.

6 Did you talk to them?

No, I didn't. Look! That's the car.

Quick! Follow them.

Thank you.

Did you notice a man and a woman?   Yes, I did.
Did they look at you?   No, they didn't.
What did they look like?   I don't know. I didn't look carefully.

① Read the story and circle.

1 Kelly (showed) / didn't show the boy a photo of Toto.

2 A car stopped / didn't stop near the boy in the morning.

3 The boy noticed / didn't notice a toucan in the car.

4 The boy looked / didn't look at Claudia's face.

5 The boy talked / didn't talk to Magnus and Claudia.

6 The boy followed / didn't follow Magnus and Claudia.

② Read and number. Then ask and answer.

One. What did he/she look like?

①    ②    ③    ④

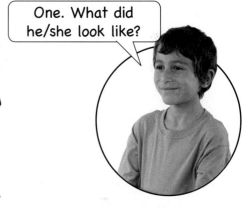

..... He was tall with a black moustache and beard.

..... She was thin with wavy brown hair and glasses.

..... He was not very tall with short blond hair and blue eyes.

..... She was pretty with long red hair and brown eyes.

③ Think and write with Dr Wild.

Look:	short/tall/thin/pretty	**Hair:**	long/short/wavy + colour
Eyes:	blue/brown/green/grey	**Other:**	beard/moustache/glasses

Think of a man or woman you remember from a film or book. What did he or she look like?

The man was tall with short brown hair, blue eyes and a moustache.

8 I'd like tickets for the museum, please.

1 **Read and write** morning, afternoon **or** evening **under the pictures.**

> **November**
>
> 17 Saturday
>
> It was cold and windy today. In the morning I walked to the park with Beth. We played on the swings and the slide in the playground. I climbed a tree and Beth watched me.
>
> After lunch we visited the Science Museum and looked at the old computers. There was a café behind the museum. Beth wanted a strawberry ice cream but I wanted a chocolate cake. The cake was delicious.
>
> There was a storm in the evening and it was horrible outside. I stayed at home and watched a film with my mum. It was about a spy with a funny moustache and beard. I liked the film but my mum didn't like it.

....

....

....

2 **Read, ask and answer.**

1 Did Harry walk to the park with Mel?

2 Did Beth climb the tree?

3 Did Harry and Beth look at old computers in the museum?

4 Did Beth want a strawberry ice cream?

5 Did Harry and his mum go to the cinema?

6 Did Harry watch a spy film with his mum?

Writing Class: *and, but*

3 **Look at the examples.**

Then look at Harry's diary again. Find and circle and in red and but in blue.

> It was sunny and there weren't any clouds in the sky.
>
> It was cloudy but it didn't rain.

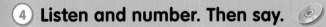
4 **Listen and number. Then say.**

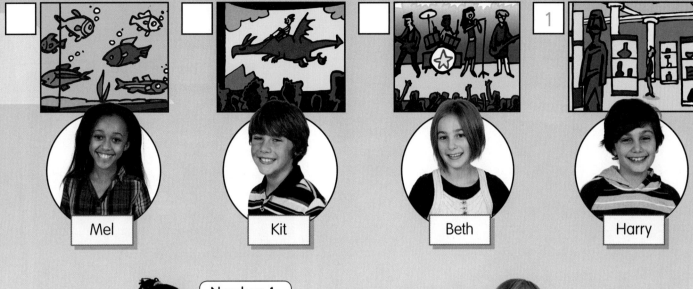

| | | | 1 |

Mel   Kit   Beth   Harry

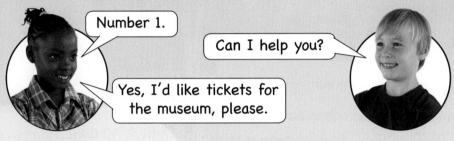

Number 1.

Can I help you?

Yes, I'd like tickets for the museum, please.

5 **Listen again and write.**

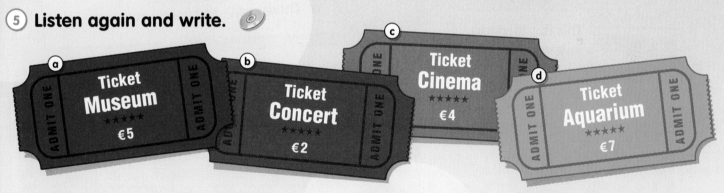

a **Ticket Museum** ★★★★★ €5

b **Ticket Concert** ★★★★★ €2

c **Ticket Cinema** ★★★★★ €4

d **Ticket Aquarium** ★★★★★ €7

1 Tickets ..2..   Euros ..10..
2 Tickets ....   Euros ....

3 Tickets ....   Euros ....
4 Tickets ....   Euros ....

6 **Choose a place from 5 and write. Then act it out.**

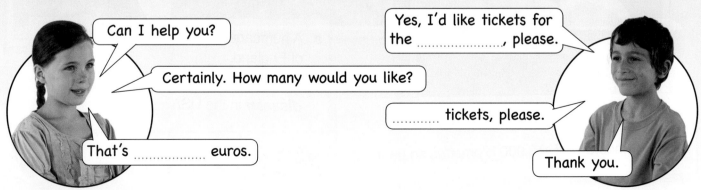

Can I help you?

Yes, I'd like tickets for the ...., please.

Certainly. How many would you like?

.... tickets, please.

That's .... euros.

Thank you.

FlyHigh File: Hurricanes

1 **Look and guess. Tick the true sentences.**

This is a **hurricane.**

a Hurricanes *last* more than a month. ....

b Hurricanes can be 1,000 kilometres across. ✔......

This is a **flood.**

a Hurricanes *cause* terrible floods. ....

b There aren't any floods in towns. ....

This is a **tornado.**

a Hurricanes can *produce* tornadoes. ......

b The winds *travel* at 3,000 kilometres an hour. ......

Winds and floods **destroy** houses.

a A hurricane destroyed the capital city of England. ......

b A hurricane caused the worst *natural disaster* in the USA. ....

A hurricane is a very big storm with heavy rain and strong winds. Hurricanes can be a thousand kilometres across. They last for more than a week. The winds are 120 to 300 kilometres an hour. Sometimes the hurricane winds produce tornadoes.

Hurricanes come between May and November when the ocean is warm. A hurricane starts over the ocean and moves from east to west. It moves about 25 kilometres every hour. When it comes on land, it causes terrible floods and people must move to a different town. Some years there are a lot of hurricanes and some years there aren't many.

Every hurricane has a name. In August 2005 there was a very strong hurricane in the USA. Its name was Katrina. The winds destroyed many houses, trees and cars and there were terrible floods, especially in the beautiful old city of New Orleans. Many people died. It was the worst natural disaster in the history of the USA.

3 Read and write True or False.

1 A hurricane is a very big snow storm. _False_

2 Hurricanes come between November and May. ....

3 Hurricanes move about 25 kilometres every hour. ....

4 There are a lot of hurricanes every year. ....

5 Every hurricane has a name. ....

6 The worst natural disaster in America was in 2005. ....

My Project

Make a weather wheel and write about the weather for a week.

My Weather Wheel

Today's Weather is:

Turn

Peter

Name

On Monday it was cold and windy.
On Tuesday it rained in the morning. In the afternoon it was cloudy.
On Wednesday it was cloudy and the sky was grey all day.
On Thursday there was a storm with thunder and lightning.
On Friday it was sunny and hot and there wasn't any wind.

The FlyHigh Review

① Say it with Aunt Sophie.

a) Listen and point. Then repeat.

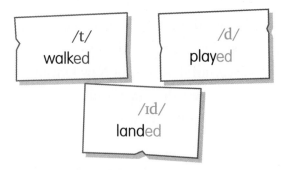

/t/
walked

/d/
played

/ɪd/
landed

b) Listen and circle. Then repeat.

1	visited	t	d	(ɪd)	6	watched	t	d	ɪd
2	washed	t	d	ɪd	7	asked	t	d	ɪd
3	lived	t	d	ɪd	8	stayed	t	d	ɪd
4	listened	t	d	ɪd	9	needed	t	d	ɪd
5	waited	t	d	ɪd					

② Write and number.

1 The person with blond hair needs a .....compass........ .

2 The person with a moustache and beard needs a ....

3 The person with long red hair and a pretty face needs a ....

4 The person with short black hair needs a ....

5 The person with wavy brown hair needs a ....

6 The person with a thin face and glasses needs  ....

a ☐

b ☐

c ☐

d 1

e ☐

f ☐

③ What about you? Choose and write.

dance ~~speak English~~ drive sing write talk swim walk
~~well~~ badly slowly quietly quickly carefully happily

1 My teacher ...speaks English well......... .

2 I ....

3 My dad ....

4 My friend ....

5 My mum ....

6 ....

④ **Read and write.**

lazy ~~helpful~~ friendly funny clever

1 He's washing the dishes and she's sweeping the floor. They're ....helpful........... .

2 Aunt Jane and Uncle Tim are working but their niece is lying in bed. She's ....

3 My nephew is telling a story and everybody is laughing. He's ....

4 The Russian girl knows a lot and she learns quickly. She's ....

5 My friend is talking to the new girl in our class. He's ....

⑤ **Listen and tick.**

1
 ☐  ☐

2
 ☐  ☐

3
 ☐  ☐

4
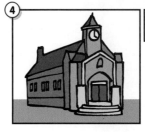 ☐ 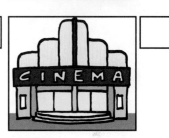 ☐

⑥ **Look and write.**

a storm with thunder and lightning   cloudy   ~~hot and sunny~~   windy and cold   a lot of snow

1 On Monday it was ....hot and sunny.. .

2 On Tuesday there was ....

3 On Wednesday there was ....

4 On Thursday it was ....

5 On Friday it was ....

Robinson Crusoe

① **Read and listen.**

PENGUIN READERS

Robinson Crusoe

Daniel Defoe

In September 1659 I leave Brazil for Africa with ten other men. It is very hot and the weather is good. But after twelve days there is a great storm. The sea plays with me for a very long time. It leaves me on the beach. I am very tired and **ill**. Where are all the other men? I don't know.

The sea is quiet now. I've got nothing with me – no food, no **tools**, no **gun** or **knife**. I swim to the ship and find many important things there: food and drink, guns, pens and paper, money, clothes, knives, books. I make a small boat and make eleven **journeys** between the beach and the ship. Then the storms start again and I stay on **land**.

The wind and rain are strong all night. The next morning I can't see the ship. It is under the sea, with my ten friends.

I am on an **island**. I find a place for my home. I make a **tent** in a **cave**. I cut down young trees and build a strong wall round my home. I have two rooms in my home. I live and sleep in the tent and I use the cave for my food and water.

There is rain every day for two months from the middle of August to the middle of October. I can't leave my house because the rain is very heavy but I am busy.

The end of September is a sad day for me. One year on this island. One year with no people and no talking. I am very quiet and sad all day.

Then one day I go to the beach and I see something **strange**. It is a man's **footprint**. How is this possible? I walk up and down the beach and look at the mark again. Strange ideas are in my head. Is there a man in the trees? Who is on my island?

I stay in my house for three days. I can't sleep. Are there other people on the island?

Glossary

....cave....	a space inside a mountain
....	you make this when you walk on the beach
....	this is something dangerous that cowboys and policemen use
....	not well
....	this is land with sea all around it
....	going from one place to another place
....	you use this to cut things
....	we live on this, fish live in the sea
....	not like things you know or see every day
....	a place to sleep in the mountains or on the beach
....	you use these to make things

farm cow grass owl pond bull

Magnus and Claudia had an accident!

1 Where are Magnus and Claudia?

I saw their car. But where is it now?

2 They went to that farm, I think! I can see a horse and some cows eating grass.

3 What was that noise?

It was an owl.

No. I heard a crash!

Magnus and Claudia had an accident!

Magnus drove into a tree!

5 They fell in the duck pond! They're wet and angry!

The ducks are angry too!

The cow is angry too!

6 That's not a cow. It's a bull!

1 Read the story and correct one word.

1 Claudia and Magnus went to a ~~shop~~. *farm*

2 Magnus walked into a tree. ....

3 They swam in a duck pond. ....

4 They were wet and happy. ....

5 There were cows, ducks, an owl, a horse and a mouse on the farm. ....

2 Listen and number.

3 Choose and write.

had ~~drove~~ fell heard saw went

Last night we **(1)** *drove* to the farm and we **(2)** .... an old woman. We asked her for a room for the night. We **(3)** .... some bread and milk and then we **(4)** .... to bed. We **(5)** .... lots of strange noises but we were tired and we **(6)** .... asleep very quickly!

10

 scared
 confused
 nervous
 unhappy

Did they find Toto?

Kelly and Jack sent some photos and an email.

Did they find Toto?

No, they didn't!

To: Harry@flyhigh.com, Beth@flyhigh.com
From: Kelly@flyhigh.com
Subject: Claudia and Magnus had an accident!

Hi all!

We saw Claudia and Magnus yesterday. They crashed their car! We didn't speak to them and we didn't find Toto. Aunt Sophie is worried. Oscar didn't like the farm and he didn't sleep well. The cows were very big and he was scared. He didn't know what the owls were. He thought they were flying cats. He was confused! The bull was very big and noisy and Oscar was nervous all night. He didn't want the bull to chase him too. Poor Oscar, he was very unhappy!
We took some photos of Claudia and Magnus yesterday. Here they are!

Hope you are all OK.

Love, Kelly and Jack

---

1 **Match and write.**

They didn't like this animal!   ~~Magnus drove very badly!~~   They didn't see the pond!

Beth: Did Claudia and Magnus have an accident?
Harry: Yes, they did. _Magnus drove very badly._

Mel: Did they fall in?
Harry: Yes, they did. ....

Beth: Did the bull chase them?
Harry: Yes, it did. ....

Learn with Oscar

Did Oscar sleep well?
No, he didn't. He didn't sleep all night.

Did he hear the owl?
Yes, he did.

(2) Choose and write.

~~nervous~~   unhappy   scared   confused

Look at all those people!

Help! I don't like big dogs.

Where do I go? Here or there?

My friend isn't talking to me today.

1 _She's nervous._   **2** ....   **3** ....   **4** ....

(3) Complete, then write four questions. Then ask and answer.

~~go~~   see   have

1 ....go........... out with your friends/to the cinema/to school
2 .... bread and honey for breakfast/a good time at school/fun
3 .... a white cat/your best friend/a funny film

1 _Did you go out with your friends yesterday?_   **3** ....

2 ....   **4** ....

Did you go out with your friends yesterday?

No, I didn't.

(4) Listen and write. Then sing.

Did   Was   see   hear   ~~have~~   laugh   dance

Did you **(1)** have a good day yesterday?
Did you sing? Did you **(2)** .... ?
Did you play?

(3) .... you talk to your friends,
And **(4)** .... with them too?

Did you look at the sky?

(5) .... it grey, was it blue?

Did you **(6)** .... the wind blowing?

Did you go to the sea?

Did you **(7)** .... the birds flying
And sitting in trees?

Did you have a good day yesterday?

Did you have a good day yesterday?

11

| well | cold | headache | sore throat | earache | ill | stomachache |

Claudia couldn't hear.

Claudia and Magnus went to a small hotel with Toto. They were ill after they fell in the duck pond. They had colds. They couldn't drive their car and they couldn't go out. They stayed in their rooms and watched TV. Magnus had a sore throat. He could speak but he couldn't eat. He was hungry and unhappy. He had a headache and he couldn't read books or sleep. Claudia had earache and she couldn't hear. She had stomachache too. She could drink water but she couldn't eat. Toto was very unhappy too. He didn't like Claudia or Magnus but he couldn't get out of his cage.

Learn with Oscar

I can sleep today.

Oscar couldn't sleep yesterday.   can   could
He could hear the owls and the bull!

---

① Read the story and tick the correct sentence.

1 a) Claudia and Magnus couldn't find their car. ......
   b) Claudia and Magnus couldn't drive their car. ✔

2 a) Claudia had a headache and Magnus
      had earache. ......
   b) Magnus had a headache and Claudia
      had earache. ......

3 a) Magnus could sleep but he couldn't speak. ......
   b) Magnus could speak but he couldn't sleep. ......

4 a) Claudia could eat but she couldn't drink. ......
   b) Claudia could drink but she couldn't eat. ......

② Label the drawing.

headache   ~~earache~~   stomachache   sore throat   cold

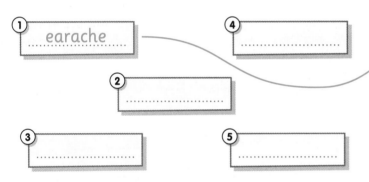

1 earache
2 ....
3 ....
4 ....
5 ....

③ Think and write with Dr Wild.

~~speak English~~   write   read   draw   sing   dance   ride a bike   swim

Think about what you could do when you were three and what you can do now.

I couldn't speak English. I can speak English now!
....
....
....
....

12 I'm sorry I couldn't come.
SKILLS

1 Read the letter and answer the questions.

1 Who is the letter to and how does it start?
2 Who is the letter from and how does it finish?
3 Where did Mel and Beth go on Saturday?

2 Read and tick the correct pictures.

Bristol
20th March

Dear Grandma,

How are you? I hope you are well.

I'm sorry I couldn't come to your birthday dinner on Sunday. I was ill.

I went to a farm with my friend Beth on Saturday. We arrived at ten o'clock in the morning. It was sunny then and I didn't wear my coat but in the afternoon it rained. There were lots of cows on the farm. Beth didn't like them. She was scared. I thought that was funny! Cows aren't dangerous! There was a horse there too. Beth can ride horses but I can't and I couldn't get on it. I fell off lots of times. She thought that was funny!

The next day I had a cold and a sore throat. I didn't go to school on Monday but I'm well again now.

I hope you had a nice time on your birthday. Seventy years old. That's great!

Send my love to Grandpa.

Love from Mel.

1

2

3

Writing Class: on, in, at ✏️

3 Look at the examples.
Then look at Mel's letter again. Find and circle on in red, in in blue and at in green.

I went to a farm on Sunday. We went for a walk in the morning. My dad took me home at six o'clock.

4 Listen and number.

5 Listen again and match. Then say.

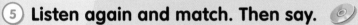

1 Harry

2 Beth

3 Mel

4 Kit

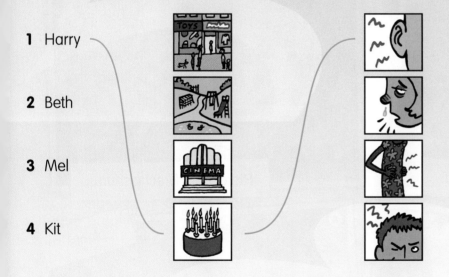

> Harry couldn't go to the party. He had earache.

6 Choose from 5 and write. Then act it out.

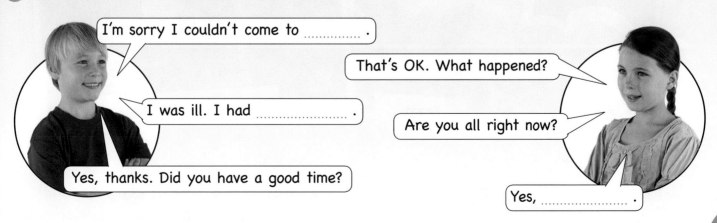

> I'm sorry I couldn't come to ....

> That's OK. What happened?

> I was ill. I had ....

> Are you all right now?

> Yes, thanks. Did you have a good time?

> Yes, ...

FlyHigh File: Dinosaurs

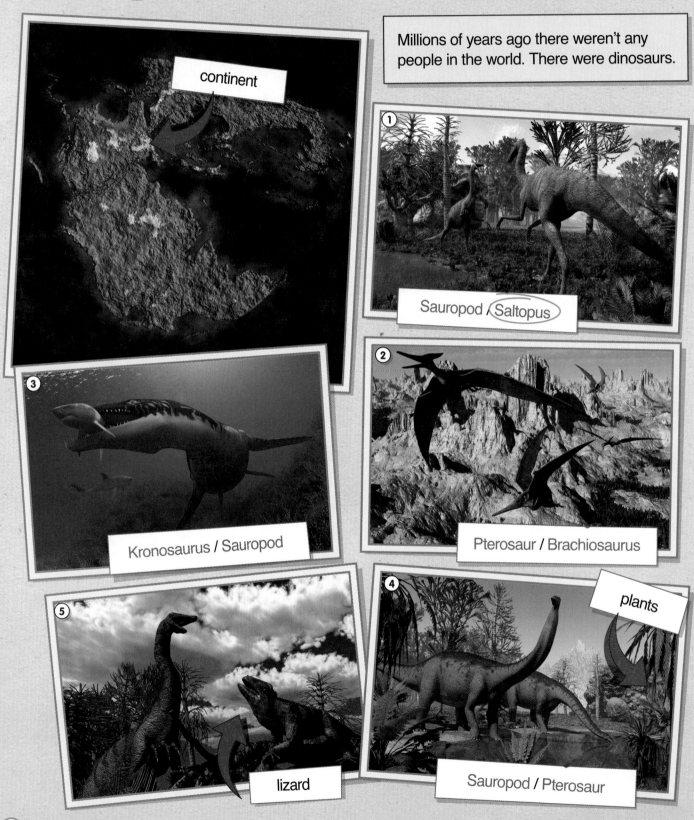

continent

Millions of years ago there weren't any people in the world. There were dinosaurs.

1 Sauropod / Saltopus

3 Kronosaurus / Sauropod

2 Pterosaur / Brachiosaurus

5 lizard

4 Sauropod / Pterosaur

plants

① Look and guess.

1 What did they eat?   **2** What could they do?   **3** Where did they live?   **4** What did they look like?

2 **Read and check. Then write the questions from 1.**

a

Where did they live?

Dinosaurs lived on every continent in the world.
Some lived on land, some in the sea and some in the sky.

b

....

Some dinosaurs ate only meat. They ate other dinosaurs! They ate dinosaur eggs too. Some dinosaurs ate only plants. They didn't eat grass; there wasn't any grass in the world then. They ate leaves. Some small dinosaurs ate lizards and insects and some ate fish.

c

....

There were many different dinosaurs.
Sauropods were giants! They had small heads and very big bodies. Pterosaurs were like huge birds. They had wings and tails. The Saltopus was small, like a chicken. We don't know what colour dinosaurs were but we think they were brown, green or yellow.

d

....

Some dinosaurs could run very fast. But some couldn't run. The Sauropods were very heavy and walked slowly.
Some, like the Kronosaurus, could swim and the Pterosaurs could fly. We think all the dinosaurs could make a lot of strange noises!

3 **Read and circle the names in the picture.**

4 **Read and write True or False.**

1 Dinosaurs ate grass. ...*False*......

2 Some dinosaurs could fly. ....

3 Some dinosaurs ate meat and eggs. ....

4 All dinosaurs could run. ....

5 All dinosaurs were big. ....

6 Dinosaurs didn't make a noise. ....

My Project

Write about the Tyrannosaurus Rex or another of your favourite dinosaurs.

The Tyrannosaurus Rex had a big head and a big body.
It ate meat and it could run.

big head

big body

ate meat
could run

big teeth

long legs

train station   road   market   castle   bridge

They went through the town.

THIEF STEALS SUITCASE

'Where did Claudia and Magnus go?' asked Jack.

'I don't know,' said Dr Wild. 'They didn't stay at the farm.'

'There's a photo in yesterday's newspaper,' said Kelly 'I think it's Magnus. He's at the train station. He's buying tickets.'

'It is Magnus. We must go to the station,' said Dr Wild. 'Have you got the map, Jack?'

'Yes, I have,' said Jack. 'We walk along this road. It goes past the market and around the castle. Then we go across the bridge.'

'Do we go through the park?' asked Kelly.

'Yes, we do,' said Jack. 'The station is opposite the park.'

Dr Wild and the children left the hotel and walked quickly to the station.

'I can see Claudia and Magnus,' shouted Jack 'They're getting on the train. Run!'

Dr Wild and the children got on the train with Oscar, and it left the station.

  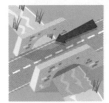  

Oscar went along the road,	past the market,	across the bridge,	around the castle and	through the park.

① Read the story and match.

1 Dr Wild and the children went past
2 They went around
3 They went across
4 They went through
5 They went to

a the park.
b the bridge.
c the train station.
d the castle.
e the market.

② Listen and tick.

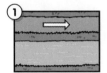
river ....

road ✔ ....

castle ....

train station ....

supermarket ......

hotel ....

bridge ....

field ....

market ....

park ....

③ Look and write.

across through around ~~past~~ along

1 The boy walked .... *past* .... the farm.

2 He walked .... the field.

3 He ran .... the forest.

4 He went .... the mountain.

5 He ran .... the beach.

41

money	seat	search	carriage	look after	luggage

How much were the tickets?

It's Jack on the phone!

Mel: Where are you?

Jack: We're on a train.

Mel: How much were the tickets?

Jack: Fifty euros.

Mel: Did you have fifty euros?

Jack: Yes, but we haven't got much money now. I've got a little but Kelly hasn't got any! We need to go to the bank soon.

Mel: Are there many people on the train?

Jack: Yes, there are a lot of people. There are only a few empty seats.

Mel: Are Claudia and Magnus on the train?

Jack: We think so. Kelly and I are searching every carriage. We hope they've got Toto with them.

Mel: What's Dr Wild doing?

Jack: She's looking after the luggage and Oscar. Oscar is drinking a little milk.

Mel: Send our love to Oscar!

Jack: We will!

① **Read and match.**

1 Where are Kelly and Jack?
2 How much were the tickets?
3 What are Kelly and Jack doing?
4 Are Claudia and Magnus on the train?
5 What's Dr Wild doing?
6 What's Oscar doing?

a She's looking after Oscar.
b He's drinking a little milk.
c They were fifty euros.
d They think so.
e They're on a train.
f They're searching every carriage.

Is there much luggage?
Are there many people?

There's a little luggage.
There isn't much luggage.
There are a few people.
There aren't many people.

② **Look and say** There isn't much …/There aren't many … .

seats   spaghetti   money   milk   carrots   tomatoes

There aren't many seats.

③ **Now circle and write** a little **or** a few.

1 There **is** / are _____a little_____ money.

2 There is / are _____ seats.

3 There is / are _____ milk.

4 There is / are _____ tomatoes.

5 There is / are _____ spaghetti.

6 There is / are _____ carrots.

④ **Listen and circle. Then sing.**

We're travelling on the train,
We're travelling on the train.
Out of the **(1)** door /(window)
what can you see,
From the train, from the train?
A **(2)** little / lot of blue sky and
(3) not many / many clouds,
From the train, from the train.
A **(4)** lot of / few people and
(5) a little / not much rain
From the train, from the train.
We're travelling on the train,
We're travelling on the train.

I heard something!

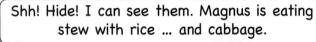

① Shh! Hide! I can see them. Magnus is eating stew with rice ... and cabbage.

Be careful or they will see you.

② What's Claudia eating?

Steak, peas and chips. She's got a lot of chips.

I'm hungry.

③ Listen. I heard something. Did you hear anything?

No, nothing.

④ Have a look. Can you see anybody?

There's nobody there.

⑤ Are you sure? I'm sure I heard somebody. Let me see!

⑥ Look at that beautiful cat! Magnus, I want that cat.

Learn with Oscar

I heard somebody.
Did you hear anybody?
There's nobody here.

I heard something.
Did you hear anything?
No, nothing.

1 **Read the story and write True or False.**

1 Jack couldn't see Magnus or Claudia. ...False........

2 Kelly didn't eat anything. ....

3 Nobody was hungry. ....

4 Claudia heard something. ....

5 Magnus didn't see anybody next to the door. ....

6 Claudia didn't want the cat. ....

2 **Look and write.**

nothing   somebody   anybody   something
anything   ~~nobody~~

1 .....Nobody..... is eating stew, rice and cabbage.

2 The man isn't eating ....

3 There's isn't .... between the man and the woman.

4 .... is eating steak, chips and peas.

5 There's .... in the glass.

6 The woman is eating ....

3 **Think and write with Dr Wild.**

writing   eating   standing up   wearing a coat   reading   sitting behind me   talking

Look at the people in your class. Write about what they are doing, using *Somebody* or *Nobody*.

Somebody is writing.
Nobody is eating.
....
....
....
....
....

16 I'd like chips.

SKILLS

① Read and number the pictures.

Our school trip to Windsor Castle

Yesterday our class went on a school trip to Windsor Castle. First we went to the train station and bought our tickets. Then we got on the train. There was nobody else in our carriage. I sat next to Mel. I like trains.

We arrived in Windsor at eleven o'clock and we walked across the road to the castle. It's very old. A man showed us around the castle. He told us many stories about the old kings and queens.

Then we had lunch. I had fish with a lot of chips and some peas. Afterwards we walked in Windsor Great Park. Finally we went to the shop and I bought a pencil. It was a wonderful day.

1

② Read and answer.

1 Where did the class go yesterday?

2 Was there anybody else in the carriage?

3 What time did the class arrive in Windsor?

4 What did Beth eat for lunch?

5 What did the class do after lunch?

6 What did Beth buy?

Writing Class : *first, then, afterwards, finally* 🖊

③ **Look at the examples.**

Then look at Beth's report again. Find and circle the adverbs.

 First we walked around the town.

 Then we ate lunch.

Afterwards we walked in the park.

Finally we went home.

4 Complete the menu.

rice   peas   cabbage   steak   milk   ice cream   chips   water   chocolate cake   pizza

a H
stew

b

c

d

e

f
bread

g

h
salad

i

j

k
orange juice

l

m

n

o
strawberries

QUEEN'S CAFE MENU

5 Listen and write H (Harry), K (Kit) or M (Mel).

6 Choose from 4 and write. Then act it out.

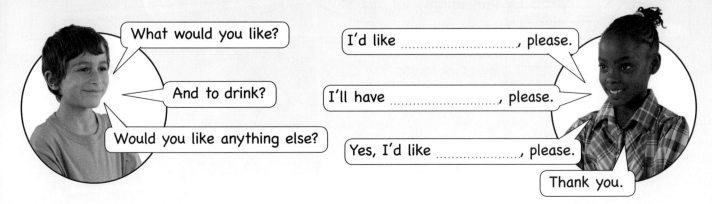

What would you like?

I'd like ...., please.

And to drink?

I'll have ...., please.

Would you like anything else?

Yes, I'd like ...., please.

Thank you.

FlyHigh File: London bus tour

1 Read about the famous places in London.

St Paul's Cathedral

This is a very old and beautiful **church**.

Tate Modern

This is a very famous modern **art gallery**.

The Tower of London.

Learn about the kings and queens of England in the Tower of London.

The London Eye

See London from the **Big Wheel**.

Big Ben and the Houses of Parliament

Big Ben is the name of the bell in the clock **tower**.

HIGH HOLBORN

ALDWYCH

THE STRAND

FLEET STREET

CANNON STREET

UPPER THAMES STREET

WATERLOO BRIDGE

WHITEHALL

VICTORIA EMBANKMENT

STAMFORD STREET

SOUTHWARK STREET

SOUTHWARK BRIDGE

LONDON BRIDGE

TOWER HILL

TOWER BRIDGE ROAD

WATERLOO ROAD

BOROUGH HIGH STREET

WESTMINSTER BRIDGE

BOROUGH ROAD

1

2 Listen and number.

3 **Read and draw the route.**

I went on a sightseeing tour around London on a double-decker bus when I was in England. It was great. We started at the Tower of London and we went across Southwark Bridge. We went along Southwark Street, past Tate Modern. That is an art gallery. We didn't go into the art gallery.

Then we went along Stamford Street, past Waterloo Bridge and stopped at the London Eye. That is a Big Wheel and we went on it. You could see all of London from the top. Then we went across Westminster Bridge. I could see Big Ben and the Houses of Parliament. We went along Whitehall, the Strand, Aldwych and Fleet Street and past St Paul's Cathedral. Then we went along Cannon Street and we finished the tour at the Tower of London again.

4 **Now answer True or False.**

1 The tour was by double-decker bus. True

2 The tour started and finished at the same place. ....

3 He walked around the art gallery. ....

4 He went across Waterloo Bridge. ....

5 He went on the London Eye. ....

My Project

Think of some interesting places in your town.
Make an information leaflet.

Come to Bridgetown!

Come and see the old castle. It's in Main Street.

In High Street there is a History Museum. There are lots of interesting things to see there.
There is a famous bridge over the river.

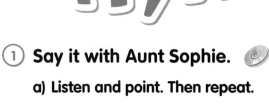

The Fly High Review

① **Say it with Aunt Sophie.**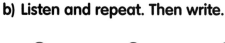

a) Listen and point. Then repeat.

/w/ window	/w/ whale

/h/ whose	/h/ horse

b) Listen and repeat. Then write.

 ① wh_ite

 ② ....otel

 ③ ....o

 ④ ....ater

 ⑤ ....avy

 ⑥ ....ole

 ⑦ ill

⑧ ....eel

② **Read and write.**

tired   worried   scared   ~~unhappy~~   confused   nervous

1 The boy didn't have any money. — He was unhappy.

2 The woman slept badly. — She was

3 Claudia didn't understand the map.

4 The girl had an exam.

5 The man couldn't see his luggage at the airport.

6 Magnus saw a big bull in front of him.

③ **Look and write the questions. Then answer with A few/A little/A lot.**

steaks   ~~chips~~   peas   ~~cabbage~~   rice   stew

①    ②    ③   ④ 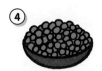   ⑤    ⑥

1 How many chips are there ? A few.

2 How much cabbage is there ? A little.

3 How ?

4 How ?

5 How ?

6 How ?

④ Listen and match. Then write and say.

stomachache   earache   headache   cold and sore throat

1 mum .... /not eat anything.

2 dad ....earache........ /not go to work.

3 brother .... /not go to school.

4 sister .... /not speak.

Her mum had an earache.
She couldn't go to work.

⑤ Circle and write.

castle   market   bridge   church   train station   road

The man drove **(1)** along / across the ...road... and **(2)** past / across the ....

Then he went **(3)** around / through the .... and **(4)** along / around the ....

He went **(5)** past / around the .... and he came to the **(6)** ....

⑥ Write.

1 I didn't drive a double-decker bus.
I ......drove......... a car.

2 I didn't go to the theatre yesterday.
I .... to the farm.

3 I didn't see the horses. I .... the cows.

4 I didn't fall in the river. I .... in the pond!

⑦ What about you? Answer.

1 Where did you go after school yesterday?
....

2 What time did you go to bed last night?
....

3 What did you eat for breakfast?
....

4 What did you do last lesson?
....

Alice in Wonderland

1 Read and listen.

PENGUIN READERS

Alice in Wonderland
Lewis Carroll

The Mad Hatter's Tea Party

There was a tree in front of the house. Under the tree was a big table with a lot of chairs round it. But there were only three at the table: the Mad Hatter, the March **Hare** and a large brown mouse. The Mouse sat between the Mad Hatter and the March Hare. It was asleep, so they talked over its head.

When they saw Alice, they cried, 'No, no, you can't sit here! There isn't a **place** for you!'

'There are a lot of places,' Alice said. She sat down in a chair at one end of the table.

'Have some **wine**,' the Mad Hatter said politely.

Alice looked round the table but there was only **tea**.

'I don't see any wine,' she answered.

'There isn't any,' said the March Hare.

'Then why did you say, "Have some wine"? It wasn't very **polite** of you,' Alice said angrily.

'We didn't invite you to tea, but you came. That wasn't very polite of *you*,' said the March Hare.

'No, it wasn't. Cut your hair!' said the Mad Hatter.

'Oh, be quiet,' said Alice.

The Mad Hatter opened his eyes very **wide** but he said nothing. Then he took out his watch and looked at it. 'What day is it?' he asked.

Alice thought for a little. 'Wednesday, I think,' she said.

'My watch says Monday,' the Mad Hatter said. 'You see, I was right. Butter isn't good for a watch.' He looked **angrily** at the March Hare.

'But it was the *best* butter,' answered the March Hare.

'Yes, but you put it in with the bread knife. Perhaps some bread got in.'

The March Hare took the watch from the Mad Hatter and looked at it sadly. Then he put it in his tea. He took it out and looked at it again. 'It was the *best* butter, you know,' he repeated.

Alice looked at the watch. 'It's a strange watch!' she said. 'It tells you the day but it doesn't tell you the time.'

'So, does your watch tell you the year?' asked the Mad Hatter.

'No,' Alice answered, 'but it's the same year for a very long time.'

'And my watch doesn't tell the time because it's always tea-time.'

Glossary

angrily	the way you speak or act when something has made you unhappy or cross
....	a big rabbit
....	where you sit or stand
....	this is when you say please and thank you
....	a hot, brown drink
....	open as much as possible
....	a red or white drink for men and women

rescue
 scarf
 glove
 jacket
 belt
 trainers
 tie

Is it yours?

1 You're safe, Oscar. You're our cat, not theirs!

Now we must rescue Toto.

2 We're at the station. Oh no! Look!

TICKETS

Don't forget your scarf.

We must get off the train.

3 Somebody dropped a glove. Is it yours?

No, it isn't mine. Is it Claudia's?

Yes, it's hers.

4 This bag isn't ours. Whose is it?

I think it's Magnus's.

5 What's in it?

There are some clothes – a jacket and a belt.

6 Anything else?

Yes, there are some trainers and a tie.

That tie is definitely his.

Learn with Oscar

I	mine
you	yours
he	his
she	hers
we	ours
they	theirs

① **Read the story and match.**

1 Whose cat is it?

2 Whose is it?

3 Whose is it?

4 Whose is it?

a It's hers.

b He isn't theirs. He's ours.

c It's his.

d It's mine.

② **Listen and match. Then write.**

① ② ③ ④ ⑤

Kelly   Jack

1 The ___scarf___, _____ and _____ are hers. **2** The _____, _____ and _____ are his.

③ **Ask and answer.**

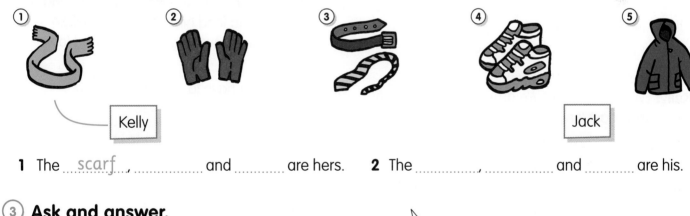

Kelly   Jack

Whose dress is it? It's hers.

Whose torch is it? It's theirs.

Whose trainers are they? They're his.

18

arrive	leave	start	lose	bring	finish

You don't have to shout!

Kit: Is there an email from Jack and Kelly?

Mel: No, there isn't but they're online. We can talk to them.

Kit : Hello. Any news?

Mel: Kit, you don't have to shout! They can hear you.

Kelly: We're in Poland. We arrived this morning at half past ten.

Jack: Claudia and Magnus got off the train and we left the train quickly.

Kelly: Magnus dropped his bag. We started to follow but we lost them. We left the bag at the station.

Mel: Have they got Toto?

Kelly: Yes, they brought Toto with them.

Jack: We have to go now. Oscar is hungry and Kelly has to feed him. Then we must go to bed. We have to get up early and look for Toto.

Mel: Yes, and I have to do my homework.

Kelly: It's very late.

Kit: It's OK. She doesn't have to finish it tonight.

Jack: That's good.

Mel: Bye.

---

① **Read and write True or False.**

1 Kelly and Jack are in Poland. ....True....

2 They arrived at half past eleven in the morning. ....

3 Claudia and Magnus stayed on the train. ....

4 Kelly and Jack lost Claudia and Magnus. ....

5 Claudia and Magnus brought Toto with them. ....

6 Kit has got some homework to do. ....

Learn with Oscar

I/You/We/They
We have to look after Oscar.
I don't have to feed him.

They have to look for Toto.
They don't have to start looking tonight.

He/She/It
Kelly has to feed him.
She doesn't have to brush him. I do.

(2) **Look and say.**

1 tidy the bedroom

2 get up early

3 feed the dog

4 walk to school

5 do homework

6 wear a uniform

They have to tidy the bedroom. He doesn't have to get up early.

(3) **Choose and write.**

bring   finishes   ~~leave~~   start   arrive

Every day, I have to **(1)** ...leave... home at eight o'clock. I **(2)** .... at school at half past eight.
My lessons **(3)** .... at nine o'clock. I don't have to **(4)** .... my lunch to school;
I can eat in the canteen. School **(5)** .... at three o'clock.

(4) **Sing. Then answer the questions for you.**

What do you have to do today?
What do you have to do?
Do you have stay at home today?
Do you have to go to school?
Do you have to do your homework?
Do you have to clean your room?

I don't have to stay at home today.
I don't have to go to school.
I don't have to do my homework.
I don't have to clean my room.
I can go to the park and play with my friends.
I can climb or ride my bike.
I can watch TV or make a cake.
I can do whatever I like.
It's Saturday afternoon.

| bank | post office | send | find | garage | hire |

Dr Wild went to the bank to get some money.

The next morning Dr Wild, Jack and Kelly were very busy. They had a lot to do. Dr Wild went to the bank to get some money. Then she went to the supermarket. She bought some bread to make sandwiches for lunch. She also bought some food for Oscar. Kelly and Jack went to the post office to send a postcard to their mum and dad. Then they ran back to find Dr Wild. They had some news.

'We saw Claudia and Magnus. They came out of that hotel with a large box.' said Kelly.

'I think Magnus had their passports.'

'Where did they go?' asked Dr Wild.

'They went across the bridge,' said Jack. 'It's the road to Ukraine. Do you think they are leaving the country?'

'I don't know,' said Dr Wild. 'But we must follow them. Let's go to the garage to hire a car.'

Learn with Oscar

Dr Wild went to the supermarket to buy some food.
She bought some fish to feed Oscar.

1 Read the story and answer.

1 Why did Dr Wild go to the bank? ...To get some money........ .

2 Why did she go to the supermarket? ....

3 Why did Kelly and Jack go to the post office? ....

4 Why did they go to the garage? ....

2 Write and match.

bank   post office   ~~garage~~   shop   café   library

1 First Claudia went to the ....garage.................   a to get some money.

2 Then she went to the ....   b to find a book about birds.

3 Next she went to the ....   c to buy a newspaper.

4 Then she went to the ....   d to hire a car.

5 After lunch she went to the ....   e to have some lunch.

6 Finally she went to the ....   f to send a parcel.

3 Think and write with Dr Wild.

swimming pool   shops   post office   café   library   cinema   bank   aquarium   park
swim   buy some chocolate   watch a film   read a book   see the fish   play football   ride my bike
buy a T-shirt   send a letter

Imagine it's Saturday. Where are you and your family going and why?

I'm going to the library to read a book.

....

....

....

I arrive at twenty to nine.

① Read. Who wrote this homework? Tick the correct picture.

8:10 ☐

12:15 ☐

1:35 ☐

6:15 ☐

My school day

Every day I walk to school. It isn't very far. I leave my house at half past eight and I arrive at ten to nine.

Our first lesson starts at five to nine. We stop for lunch at quarter past twelve. I bring a lunch box from home. We don't have to bring a lunch box; we can eat lunch in the canteen.

After lunch I play with my friends in the playground. Lessons start again at one o'clock. School finishes at ten past three. Sometimes I have lessons after school. On Mondays I have a guitar lesson at quarter to four. On Thursday's I have a swimming lesson at half past five. Some days I have to go shopping with my mum.

② Look and match.

1 My first lesson starts. __b__
2 We finish school. ....
3 I have a guitar lesson. ....
4 I have a swimming lesson. ....

a   b   c   d

Writing Class: writing the time

③ Look at the examples.

Then look at Kit's composition again. Circle, write and draw clocks.

It's ten past eight.

It's quarter to nine.

4 Listen and match.

① Kit	② Harry	③ Mel	④ Beth
ⓐ	ⓑ	ⓒ	ⓓ

5 Listen again and draw.

After school activities

	Place	Activity	Time
1	Music room	Guitar lesson	(clock)
2	Playing field	Football match	(clock)
3	Swimming pool	Swimming lesson	(clock)
4	School hall	Dance lesson	(clock)

6 Choose from 4 and write. Then act it out.

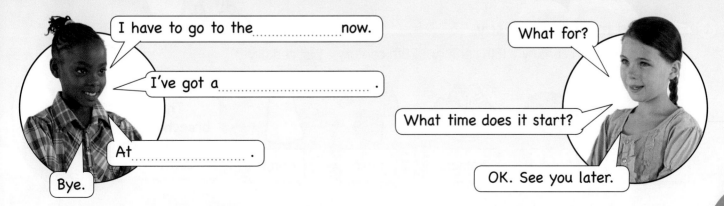

I have to go to the .... now.

What for?

I've got a ....

What time does it start?

At ....

OK. See you later.

Bye.

FlyHigh File: Clothes through the ages

1 Complete the time line.

21st   seventeenth   16th   14th   eleventh   twentieth

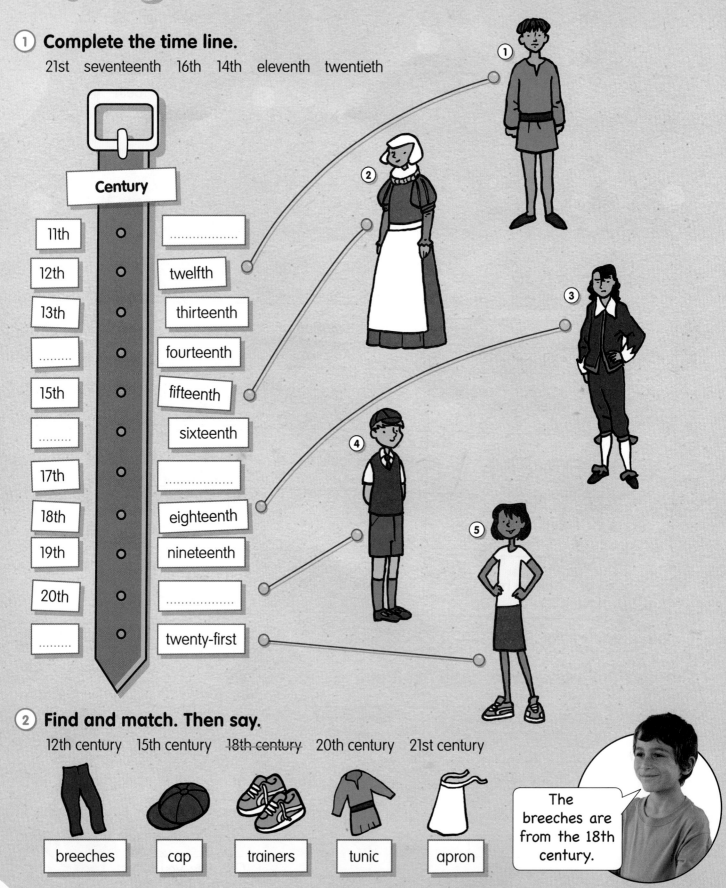

Century

11th	....
12th	twelfth
13th	thirteenth
....	fourteenth
15th	fifteenth
....	sixteenth
17th	....
18th	eighteenth
19th	nineteenth
20th	....
....	twenty-first

2 Find and match. Then say.

12th century   15th century   ~~18th century~~   20th century   21st century

breeches   cap   trainers   tunic   apron

The breeches are from the 18th century.

3 Read and check.

For hundreds of years children's clothes in Europe didn't change much. Clothes stayed the same from the fifth to the twelfth century. Boys in the twelfth century wore a short tunic with a belt and trousers. Girls wore trousers with a long dress on top.

From the fourteenth century girls wore a dress with a belt, and a cap on their head. They often wore aprons to keep their dresses clean. Boys wore a shirt, a belt, trousers and boots or pointed shoes. Poor children didn't always have shoes.

From the sixteenth to the eighteenth century children wore the same clothes as men and women. The girls wore long dresses. The boys wore dresses too until they were seven years old. Then they wore a shirt, a jacket and short trousers called breeches, with long socks and shoes. Until the end of the nineteenth century most children had only one new dress or shirt a year.

After 1900 there were many different fashions. The boy wearing a cap, shorts, a shirt and a jacket lived in the twentieth century. This is his school uniform. He is ready to go to school. The twenty-first century girl is wearing a T-shirt, skirt and trainers. These are her casual clothes.

4 Answer the questions.

1 Did fashion change from the fifth to the twelfth century?

2 When did boys wear a short tunic with a belt and trousers?

3 Did girls and women wear the same fashion in the seventeenth century?

4 How old were boys when they wore trousers in the eighteenth century?

5 How many new dresses did girls have a year in the nineteenth century?

6 Did fashion change much in the twentieth century?

My Project

Draw and write about your favourite clothes and when you wear them.

My favourite clothes are a skirt and a T-shirt. My favourite skirt is white and my favourite T-shirt is blue with a picture of a horse on it. My mum and dad gave me the T-shirt for my birthday because I like horses. I wear these clothes when I go to parties.

van

motorbike

fire engine

scooter

helicopter

The red van is faster!

1. The white van is bigger than the red one.

The red one is smaller but it's faster.

The red van, please!

2. Claudia and Magnus are on a motorbike!

Go faster, Aunt Sophie!

Yes. It's faster than our van!

3. Be careful! There's a fire engine behind us!

There's a scooter in front! Go slower, Aunt Sophie!

4. They're stopping!

Good. We're at the airport. There are lots of helicopters.

5. Are they getting into the new helicopter?

No, they're getting into the older one.

6. I'm a pilot. Come on. We need a helicopter too!

Name : Sophie Wild
Age : 30
Hair : Brown
Nationality : British

PILOT

Home Town : Bristol
Hobbies : Flying planes, reading, sport.

Learn with Oscar

The yellow helicopter is older than the green one.

old	older
big	bigger
happy	happier

① Read the story and write True or False.

1 The white van is slower than the red one. ...True..

2 The red van is bigger than the white one. ....

3 The van is faster than the motorbike. ....

4 The motorbike is smaller than the van. ....

5 The yellow helicopter is bigger than the green one. ....

6 The green helicopter is newer than the yellow one. ....

② Listen and tick the correct picture. Then look and say.

GREAT TRANSPORT RACE

I can see three vans and a scooter.

Picture 1.

③ Look at Picture 2 in 2. Circle.

1 The black scooter is (older)/ slower than the blue one.

2 The green motorbike is slower / faster than the yellow one.

3 The yellow motorbike is slower / faster than the white van.

4 The white van is cleaner / smaller than the motorbikes.

5 The man is taller / bigger than the woman.

6 The woman is happier / dirtier than the man.

 silly
 catch
 runner
 noisy
 light

They are the silliest people in the world!

Kelly: We couldn't catch Claudia and Magnus at the airport.

Beth: Jack is the fastest runner in our school!

Kelly: Yes but they got in their helicopter first. I think they're the silliest people in the world. They didn't choose the fastest one! They chose the slowest, heaviest, oldest, noisiest one. Dr Wild is a pilot and we got the fastest, lightest and quietest helicopter.

Beth: Can you see Toto?

Kelly: Yes! I think he's the saddest bird in the world at the moment. We have to catch Claudia and Magnus! It's amazing up here. We can see the River Danube.

Beth: Is that the longest river in Europe?

Harry: No. The Volga is longer.

Beth: How's Oscar?

Kelly: He's really happy. He thinks he's a helicopter pilot. He's the funniest cat in the world!

① **Read and circle.**

1 He runs very fast.   **a** Jack   **b** Magnus

2 They are very silly.   **a** Oscar and Toto   **b** Claudia and Magnus

3 It is old and heavy.   **a** the green helicopter   **b** the yellow helicopter

4 He is very sad.   **a** Toto   **b** Oscar

5 It is very long.   **a** the green helicopter   **b** the river

Learn with Oscar

fast	fastest
big	biggest
noisy	noisiest

I'm a fast runner. Kelly is faster than me. Jack is the fastest runner!

(2) Choose and write.

runner   heavy   noisy   light   ~~silly~~

1 I don't like clowns. I think they're ..... silly ....

2 She's a good .... She came first in the race at school.

3 My school bag has got ten books in it. It's really ....

4 I haven't got any books in my bag. It's ....

5 My brother is playing the drums. I can't hear you. It's very .... !

(3) Write and match. Then ask and answer.

1 high   The .. highest .. mountain is ⌐   **a** Vatican City.

2 long   The .... river is   └   **b** Mount Everest.

3 fast   The .... animal is   **c** Russia.

4 big   The .... animal is   **d** the cheetah.

5 small   The .... country is   **e** the Nile.

6 big   The .... country is   **f** the blue whale.

What's the highest mountain in the world?

Mount Everest.

(4) Listen and write. Then sing.

sweeter   ~~cleverest~~   bigger   funnier   faster   cleverest

He's a little bit lazy and a little bit fat,
But we think Oscar is the **(1)** .. cleverest ..... cat!
Other cats are **(2)** ...., they run **(3)** .... too
But other cats can't do what Oscar can do.
He's **(4)** .... than them and he's **(5)** .... too.
He always makes us laugh when we're sad and blue.
He's a little bit silly and he can't catch mice,
But we don't mind because we think he's very nice.
He's a little bit lazy and a little bit fat.
But we think Oscar is the **(6)** .... cat!

expensive   soft   comfortable   modern   dangerous   exciting   tobogganing

Oscar has got the most comfortable bed!

'What a beautiful place!' said Kelly. They were in the mountains and there was lots of snow.

'Where are we now?' asked Jack.

'We're in Ukraine,' said Dr Wild. 'Where are Claudia and Magnus?'

'They went into that big hotel,' said Jack.

'They've got more money than us!' said Kelly.

'Yes,' said Dr Wild. 'We haven't got much money. That hotel is the most expensive in the town.'

'I think this hotel is better,' said Jack.

'It's more comfortable too,' said Kelly. 'Look at Oscar. He's got the softest bed! It's the most comfortable!'

'This hotel is more modern too,' said Jack. 'There's a computer in every bedroom.'

'Look at those people skiing,' said Kelly. 'It's exciting.'

'I like tobogganing better,' said Jack. 'I think it's more exciting than skiing. Skiing is more dangerous too.'

Learn with Oscar

Jack's bed is comfortable. Kelly's bed is more comfortable. My bed is the most comfortable!

Jack's bed is soft. Kelly's bed is softer. My bed is the softest!

cheap	expensive
cheaper	more expensive
the cheapest	the most expensive

① **Read the story and write True or False.**

1 Dr Wild has got more money than Claudia and Magnus. ...False......

2 Hotel Trendy is more expensive than Hotel Posh. ....

3 Hotel Posh is more modern than Hotel Trendy. ....

4 Kelly's bed is the most comfortable. ....

5 Skiing is more dangerous than tobogganing. ....

② **Choose and write.**

~~exciting~~   expensive   modern   comfortable

1 Skiing is ...more exciting... than walking.

Tobogganing is ...the most exciting... .

2 The car is .... than the scooter.

The motorbike is ....

3 The red shoes are .... than the blue ones.

The white shoes are ....

4 The blue phone is .... than the black one.

The purple phone is ....

③ **Think and write with Dr Wild.**

cheapest   most interesting   most exciting   most dangerous

Think about different sports and write.

I think motorbike racing is the most dangerous sport.

Which bike do you like best?

I'm going to Cycle World to buy a nice, new bike!

① **Read and complete. Write the names of the bikes.**

COME TO CYCLE WORLD

ONLY €210

Red Storm

ONLY €450

King of the Road

Sunny Friend

ONLY €99.99

wheel   gears   handle – bars   brake   saddle

(1) .... is the biggest bike in the shop. It isn't the fastest bike but it's the most comfortable with a nice, big, black saddle and handlebars – and a fabulous, big, yellow basket for all your books!

(2) .... is the most modern bike we've got. It's brilliant! It's got a comfortable, small, blue saddle and with twenty-seven gears it's the fastest bike in the shop. With this bike you can go faster than all your friends!

Do you want a really amazing bike? Then **(3)** .... is for you! This fantastic, small, red bike has got stronger brakes than all the others and better and bigger lights too. It's not the cheapest bike in the shop but we think it's the best!

② **Look, read and answer.**

1 Which bike is the cheapest? ..Sunny..Friend..

2 Which bike is the fastest? ....

3 Which bike is the most comfortable? ....

4 Which bike is the most modern? ....

5 Which bike has got the biggest lights?

....

6 Which bike is the most expensive?

....

Writing Class: adjective order

③ **Look at the examples.**

Then look at the advertisement again. Find and write the adjectives in the correct order.

Opinion   Size   Colour

It's got a comfortable, small, blue saddle.

SALE SALE SALE SALE
DESIRABLE TRAINERS
BUY NOW-PRICES BELOW!

€87

€45

€215

€150

4 **Write the prices in order.**

Most expensive   €215 ....   Cheapest

5 **Listen, circle and write.**

Mel thinks …

1 the yellow / (pink) ones are most comfortable.

2 the white / yellow ones are the most modern.

3 the purple / white ones are the strongest.

4 the yellow / purple ones are the biggest and highest.

5 she can only buy the .... ones.

6 **Choose and write. Then act it out.**

more comfortable   more expensive   cheaper   stronger   heavier
more modern   more exciting   smaller   bigger   lighter

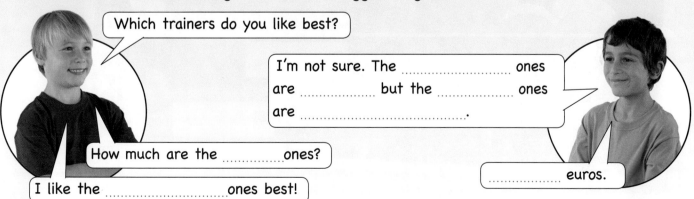

Which trainers do you like best?

I'm not sure. The .... ones are .... but the .... ones are ....

How much are the .... ones?

.... euros.

I like the .... ones best!

FlyHigh File: Planets

① Look and guess.

1 Do you know the names of the planets?
2 Which is the hottest?
3 Which is the coldest?
4 Which is the smallest?
5 Which is the biggest?

Did you know that the sun is a very big, very hot star? It gives lots of energy to nine planets and those planets are in our solar system.

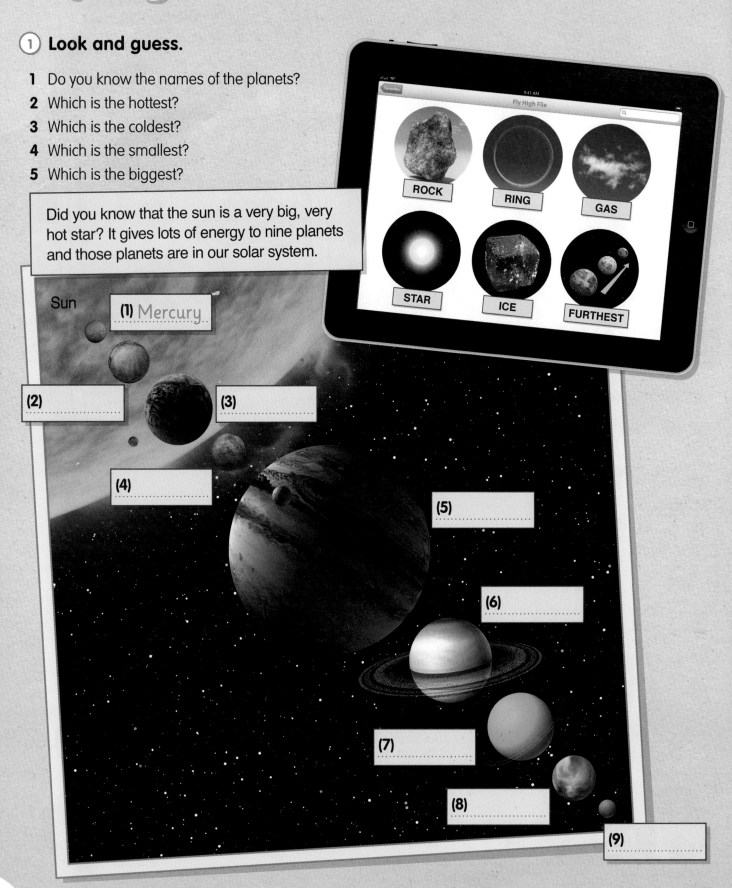

ROCK
RING
GAS
STAR
ICE
FURTHEST

Sun

(1) Mercury

(2)

(3)

(4)

(5)

(6)

(7)

(8)

(9)

② Read and check. Then label the planets.

The planet nearest to the sun is Mercury. It's the fastest planet. It goes around the sun very quickly. But it is not the hottest planet. Venus is the hottest planet and it is second nearest to the sun. The third planet is Earth. It's the most beautiful planet in the solar system. The next planet is Mars. It's smaller than Earth.

The first four planets are made of rock. Next to Mars is the biggest planet, Jupiter. It's made of gas, not rock. Jupiter hasn't got one moon like Earth, it's got sixteen! The planet with the most moons is Saturn. It's got more than sixty moons! It's the sixth furthest from the sun and there are rings round it. They're rings of ice!

Next is Uranus. It's four times bigger than Earth. Then comes Neptune. It's blue and beautiful. There are often storms on Neptune. The last planet, furthest from the sun, is Pluto. Pluto is the smallest planet. It's smaller than our moon and it's the coldest planet too. Some people think Pluto isn't a planet because it's very small.

③ Read and write the name of the planet.

Which planet ...

1 is nearest to the sun? Mercury

2 is furthest from the sun? ....

3 is the fastest? ....

4 is the stormiest? ....

5 has got the most moons? ....

6 is the most beautiful? ....

My Project

Choose a planet and write about it.

	Jupiter	Venus	Neptune	
Made of	gas	rock	gas	
Temperature	very cold	hot	very cold	
Other information	16 moons	cloudy	very stormy	

Neptune is a beautiful, blue planet.
It's made of gas and it's very cold.
It's very stormy.

The FlyHigh Review

1 **Say it with Aunt Sophie.**

a) Listen and point to the silent letter. Then repeat.

A u t u m n

W e d n e s d a y

h o u r

b) Listen and circle the silent letter. Then repeat.

① c a s t l e

② k n o w

③ c l i m b

④ w a l k

⑤ w r i t e

⑥ i s l a n d

⑦ l i g h t

⑧ g h o s t

2 **What about you? Circle and write.**

do ~~get up~~ catch go wear bring

1 I have to / don't have to .....get up..... early on school days.

2 I have to / don't have to .... a bus to school.

3 I have to / don't have to .... a tie at school.

4 I have to / don't have to .... money for my lunch to school.

5 We have to / don't have to .... homework every day.

6 I have to / don't have to .... to bed early.

3 **Write the questions. Then complete the answers.**

belt trainers ~~gloves~~ jacket

1 .....Whose are they?.....

They're my .....gloves..... . They're .....mine..... .

2 .....Whose is it?.....

It's her .... It's ....

3 ....

It's his .... It's ....

4 ....

They're our .... They're ....

①

②

③

④

4 **Look, choose and write.**

To do...
- look at the pictures
- ~~get some money~~
- have lunch
- send a letter
- hire a van
- buy a scarf

1 The man went to the bank to get some money .

2 He went to .

3 .

4 .

5 .

6 .

5 **Write.**

1 Police cars are _faster_
(fast) than fire engines.

2 Taxis are
(expensive) than buses.

3 Motorbikes are
(noisy) than scooters.

4 Trains are
(comfortable) than buses.

5 Helicopters are
(exciting) than planes.

6 Vans are
(big) than cars.

6 **Write true sentences.**

1 Hydrogen is/light gas
Hydrogen is the lightest gas.

2 Pluto is/far planet in the solar system

3 Hippos are/dangerous animals in the world

4 Earth is/beautiful planet in the solar system

5 Ducks have got/soft feathers

The Prince and the Pauper

① **Read and listen.**

PENGUIN READERS

The Prince and the Pauper

Mark Twain

Every day Tom went to the **palace** where the King of England lived. Tom was **poor** and he **begged** on the way and sometimes got money. More often he got a kick.

Then one day Tom saw a boy in the palace. He looked at the boy's beautiful clothes and he knew. It was Prince Edward, the king's son! He ran to the **gates**.

'I want to see the prince,' he cried.

One of the **soldiers** hit Tom. Tom fell and everybody laughed. But the prince saw and was very angry.

'Why did you hit that poor boy?' he shouted at the soldiers. 'Open the gates. Bring him in.'

'But sir …,' said the soldier. 'He's only a poor, dirty **beggar**.'

'My father is king of **rich** people and poor people,' answered Prince Edward. 'Bring in the boy.'

The prince took Tom inside the palace, up some stairs and into one of his rooms.

'Are you hungry?' he asked.

'I'm always hungry, sir,' answered Tom.

Edward called a **servant**.

'Bring some food,' he ordered. 'Meat, cake, fruit and bread.'

The servant brought food and Tom ate.

'Now, who are you?' asked the prince. 'I see you at the palace gates every day. I watch you from the window.'

'My name is Tom Canty, sir. I live with my family in a room near London Bridge.'

'In a room?'

'Yes − with my mother, my father, my grandmother and my two sisters. Our room is quite big and it is very **cheap**.'

'Why do you all live in one room?'

'Because we're very poor,' said Tom. 'My father doesn't work and I have to beg for money.'

'I have two sisters too but they don't play with me and I don't know any boys. Do you play with other boys?'

'Yes, of course. We play by the river and we swim. Sometimes we play princes and soldiers. I'm always the prince,' said Tom.

Edward was sad. 'I would like to be a poor boy,' he said. 'I would like to play with other boys.'

Then Edward had an idea. He jumped out of his chair. 'Let's change clothes. You can be the prince and I'll be the **pauper**.'

Edward put on Tom's old, thin trousers and shirt. Tom washed his face and hands. They had the same eyes, the same nose, the same hair. Tom put on Edward's fine clothes and shoes.

'Wait here!' said the prince. 'I'm going to be a pauper for a day. I'm going to the river to swim.'

He ran out of the room.

'What shall I do?' shouted Tom.

But there was no answer.

Glossary

beg .... to ask someone you don't know for money

.... this person asks for money

.... something that doesn't cost much money is this

.... metal doors to a garden or palace

.... a big house for kings or queens

.... someone who has little or no money

.... someone with little money is this

.... someone with a lot of money is this

.... this person works in the house of a king or queen

.... this person fights for his country

25

 join in

 fancy dress

 costume

 alien

superhero

pop star

I want to join in.

Everyone's wearing fancy dress.

Look at all the people! Can you see Claudia and Magnus?

There are a lot of different costumes!

Look at that alien with a spy.

I want to join in.

Can we, Aunt Sophie?

Yes, OK, but don't forget we want to find Claudia and Magnus.

Great! I want to be a superhero.

I want to be a pop star.

I love these costumes.

Look! Oscar wants to go tobogganing!

Wow! He *is* tobogganing.

I/You/We/They	He/She/It
I want to go tobogganing.	He wants to go fast.

① Read the story and match.

1 They want to find
2 Kelly wants to wear
3 She wants to be
4 Jack wants to be
5 They want to join
6 Oscar wants to go

a tobogganing.
b a superhero.
c in the fun.
d a pop star.
e Claudia and Magnus.
f a costume.

② Listen and match. Then write.

1

Mel wants to be an .....alien...................... .

2

Harry wants to be a................................. .

3

Beth wants to be a................................. .

4

Kit wants to be a................................. .

③ Ask and answer.

have a drink   make a phone call   ~~go tobogganning~~   eat an ice cream   take the cat home   take photos

What does Oscar want to do?

He wants to go tobogganing.

26

 ice skating
 surfing
 skateboarding
 rock climbing
 cycling
 fishing

He likes tobogganing!

1 **Read and write the names.**

1 ....Kit.........

2 ....

3 ....

4 ....

Beth: Kelly and Jack sent us some more photos yesterday.

Mel: There's a funny photo of Oscar on a toboggan.

Kit: He's the funniest cat in the world! He likes tobogganing!

Beth: I like tobogganing too. It's fun. I love winter sports. I like skiing and ice skating too.

Mel: You're good at ice skating, Beth.

Beth: Thank you.

Mel: I like going to the beach. I enjoy swimming and surfing.

Beth: You like skateboarding and rollerblading too.

Mel: True.

Harry: I like climbing. I'm happy when I'm climbing trees.

Beth: Do you like rock climbing too, Harry?

Harry: Yes, I do but it's difficult. What about you, Kit?

Kit: I like cycling and fishing. Last weekend I went to the mountains with my dad. We went cycling in the morning and fishing in the afternoon. I caught a bicycle wheel! I'm not very good at fishing.

Learn with Oscar

Oscar **likes** tobogganing.
He's **good at** making friends.
He's **happy when** he's playing with Jack and Kelly.

2 **Ask and answer. Then ask and answer about you.**

Does Kit like playing basketball?

Does Mel like swimming?

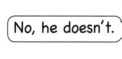

No, he doesn't.

Yes, she does.

3 **Circle and write.**

1 She (is)/ isn't good at *skateboarding* .   **3** He is / isn't good at ....

2 She is / isn't good at ....   **4** He is / isn't good at ....

4 **Listen and write. Then sing.**

sleeping   drinking   morning   somebody   ~~eating~~

I'm happy when I'm **(1)** *eating*
a lovely juicy fish.
I'm happy when I'm **(2)** ....
milk from my dish.
I'm happy when I'm **(3)** ....
in my comfortable bed.

I'm happy when **(4)** ....
is stroking my head.
I'm happy in the **(5)** ....
and in the evening too.
But most of all I'm happy
when I'm with you.

 use
 escape
 reach
 borrow
 hold

What shall we do?

Jack: Oh no! Did you see? Magnus was the alien! Claudia was the spy!

Kelly: They've got Oscar!

Jack: What shall we do now? They're halfway down the mountain.

Dr Wild: We have to rescue Oscar.

Jack: What about using the helicopter?

Dr Wild: No time for that! They're escaping! We must stop them before they reach the town.

Kelly: What about skiing after them?

Dr Wild: I'm not very good at skiing.

Kelly: Shall we ask the other people to help?

Dr Wild: Yes! That's a good idea.

Kelly: Excuse me, can you help us? That man and woman have got our cat! We have to catch them.

Man: That's terrible. You can borrow our toboggan.

Jack: Thank you.

Man: Shall I hold it for you?

Kelly: Yes. Thank you.

Dr Wild: Are we all on?

Kelly: Yes, we are.

Dr Wild: Off we go! Everybody to the rescue!

① **Read the story, circle and match.**

1 What shall we (do) / doing   **a** the helicopter?

2 What about use / using   **b** the toboggan for you?

3 What about ski / skiing after   **c** the other people to help?

4 Shall we ask / asking   **d** now?

5 Shall I hold / holding   **e** Claudia and Magnus?

② **Read and circle.**

Look, Claudia. Those children are following us. They're **(1)** (using) / doing a toboggan. They want to **(2)** ask / rescue the cat. What shall we do?

Go faster. I'm **(3)** stopping / holding the cat and it can't **(4)** rescue / escape! We must **(5)** reach / catch the town before they do and hide. Then tonight, we can **(6)** help / borrow a car and drive away.

③ **Think and write with Dr Wild.**

play football/tennis/basketball/volleyball/computer games
go to the swimming pool/park/cinema/for a walk/watch TV/listen to music/make a cake

Think about what you can do at the weekend. Write suggestions for your friend.

Hi ....

I've got some ideas for this weekend.

Shall we play football on Saturday morning?

....

....

....

28 SKILLS Shall we meet in the park or at my house?

① Read and tick the activities in the email.

To: Kit@flyhigh.com

From: Harry@flyhigh.com

Subject: Where shall we meet?

Hi Kit,

Thanks for your email. I'm very excited that you can come and stay for the weekend.
Shall we meet in the park or at my house?
We can have lunch at my house. What shall we do after lunch? Do you want to play football or go fishing? I know you like fishing and there's a lake near my house. You can use my dad's fishing rod and I can borrow one from my friend. In the evening we can watch a film or what about playing computer games? I've got the Winter Games Wii. I like playing the ice skating game but I'm not very good at it.
Have you got any DVDs or computer games? Can you bring them with you, please?

See you soon.

Harry

② Read and circle.

1 Kit can come and stay for   **a** Saturday and Sunday.   **b** the week.

2 They can have lunch   **a** at Kit's house.   **b** at Harry's house.

3 Harry wants Kit to bring   **a** the Winter Games Wii.   **b** some DVDs.

Writing Class: using *or* in questions

③ Look at the examples.

Then look at Harry's email again. Circle *or* and say the alternatives.

Have you got any DVDs or computer games? Do you want to watch a film or play computer games?

Listen and number.

5 **Listen again and circle. Then write.**

1 Kit wants to go   ....rollerblading........... today.

2 Harry wants to go   .... today.

3 Mel wants to go   .... today.

6 **Choose a holiday and activities from 4 and write. Then act it out.**

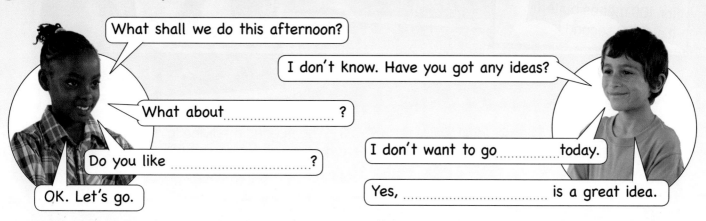

What shall we do this afternoon?

I don't know. Have you got any ideas?

What about .... ?

I don't want to go .... today.

Do you like .... ?

Yes, ... is a great idea.

OK. Let's go.

FlyHigh File: Sporting legends

This is **Lionel Messi**. He's one of the best football players in the world.

He scores a goal nearly every game.

GOAL!

This is **Michael Phelps**. He's one of the best swimmers in history.

He holds the world record for 100 metres butterfly. It's 49.82 seconds.

Olympic flag

gold medal

1 **Look and guess.**

1 Who eats eight eggs, cheese, toast, pancakes and cereal for breakfast?

2 Who lives in Spain?

3 Who needed medicine to grow when he was eleven years old?

4 Who has got very big feet?

2 Read and check.

Lionel Messi always wanted to be a football player. He was born in Argentina in 1987 and he played for his first team in 1992 when he was five years old.

By eleven he was very good at football but there was a problem. He was short and he wasn't growing taller. He needed medicine to grow but it was expensive. When he was thirteen, his family moved to Spain and the Barcelona football club paid for his medicine.

Today he plays for FC Barcelona and for Argentina. He's a brilliant goal scorer and one of the best football players in the world.

Michael Phelps is an amazing American swimmer. When he was fifteen, he competed in the 2000 Olympics. The same year he broke a world record. He's got fourteen Olympic gold medals – more than anybody in the world. He wants to win more medals so he works very hard. Every day he swims for about five hours.

He's tall with a long body and big feet and he needs to eat a lot. He eats a very big breakfast. He likes eating lots of pasta and sandwiches for lunch. For dinner he has another enormous meal. He eats the same as five men every day.

He loves his sport and he's happy when he's swimming. Some people think he's the best swimmer in history.

3 Read and answer.

1 Where was Lionel Messi born? ....Argentina....

2 How old is he? ....

3 How did Barcelona help him? ....

4 What teams does Messi play for? ....

5 What nationality is Michael Phelps? ....

6 What did he do when he was fifteen years old? ....

7 How many Olympic gold medals has Michael Phelps got? ....

8 How much does Michael Phelps eat every day? ....

My Project

Find out and write about a sporting legend from your country.

I love ice skating and I'm quite good at it. I go to the ice rink every day after school and train for an hour. I want to be as good as Oksana Domnina and Maxim Shabalin. They're Russian ice dancers. They won the World Championship for ice dancing in 2010.

29

 knock over
 lamp
 curtain
 rug
 sofa
 cushion
 prison

I'm going to phone the police!

I'm going to hide!

Learn with Oscar

I
I'm going to hide.

He/She/It
She's going to call the police.

We/You/They
They're going to go to prison.

1 **Read the story and correct one word.**

1 Dr Wild is going to ~~help~~ the police. ..... *phone* .....

2 Jack is going to sleep upstairs. ....

3 Claudia and Kelly are behind the curtains. ....

4 Toto is playing behind a cushion. ....

5 Claudia and Magnus are going to go to school. ....

2 **Listen and circle. Then look and say.** 💿

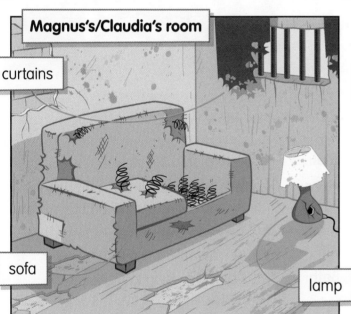

Magnus's/Claudia's room

curtains

sofa

lamp

Magnus's/Claudia's room

table

rug

cushion

chair

Claudia has got a curtain. She hasn't got a sofa.

3 **Choose and write. Then match.**

to have   ~~to phone~~   to give   to write

ⓐ

ⓑ

ⓒ

ⓓ

1 She 's going *to phone* Sally at the zoo. c

2 They .... going .... to their friends. ....

3 I .... going .... Toto some food water. .....

4 He .... going .... some milk. .....

30

plan

picnic

invitation

banner

Are they going to come home now?

Harry: Jack and Kelly have got Toto!

Kit: That's great!

Mel: Are they going to come home now?

Harry: Yes, they are but they aren't going to travel by train.

Kit: Are they going to fly home?

Harry: Yes, I think so.

Kit: Is Dr Wild going to take Toto to the zoo?

Harry: Yes, she is. Shall we have a party for them?

Mel: Yes! Let's plan a big picnic!

Harry: Yes, let's have a picnic. We can go to the park, take lots of food and then play games. Good idea!

Kit: Are you going to make a cake, Beth?

Beth: Yes, I am! I'm going to make a big chocolate cake!

Kit: I'm going to send invitations to all our friends.

Beth: I'm going to make a Welcome Home banner!

① **Read and write True or False.**

1 Jack and Kelly are going to go home. _True_

2 They are going to travel by train. _____

3 Dr Wild is going to take Toto to the zoo. _____

4 Harry and his friends are going to plan a party for Jack and Kelly. _____

5 Mel is going to send invitations to all their friends. _____

6 Beth is going to make a cake and a banner. _____

Learn with Oscar

I	He/She/It	We/You/They
Am I going to see my friends again? Yes, I am.	Is he going to fly home? Yes, he is.	Are they going to go by train? No, they aren't.
I'm not going to go to school.	He isn't going to go by train.	They aren't going to fly in a plane.

(2) **Write Yes or No for you. Then ask and answer.**

(3) **Circle and write.**

~~have~~ make eat drink write make

1 They **are** / aren't going to ..*have*.. a picnic.

2 The boy is / isn't going to .... a banner.

3 The girl is / isn't going to .... a cake.

4 Dad is / isn't going to .... invitations.

5 They are / aren't going to .... sandwiches.

6 They are / aren't going to .... milk.

(4) **Listen and circle. Then sing.**

Are you going to **(1)** come / be to our party?
It's going to **(2)** look / be just great.
We're going to **(3)** make / have a picnic.
Please come and don't be late!

We're going to **(4)** get / make some pizza.
We've got lots of **(5)** things / work to do.
It's going to **(6)** be / have such wonderful fun
And Toto is going to **(7)** fly / come too!

rare   robber   steal   jewellery   valuable   painting   diamond

Why did they want Toto?

Policeman: Claudia and Magnus are going to go to prison. They aren't going to come out for a long time!

Dr Wild: Why did they want Toto and Oscar, officer?

Policeman: Because Claudia collects rare birds and she liked Oscar!

Kelly: Why didn't they buy a cat and a toucan?

Policewoman: Because Claudia and Magnus are robbers.

Policeman: They never buy anything, they always steal things. We found lots of jewellery and valuable paintings in their house in Switzerland.

Policewoman: There were lots of valuable diamonds too!

Dr Wild: Thank you for your help, officer.

Policeman: Thank you, Dr Wild, and thank you, Kelly and Jack. You were very brave and helpful.

Dr Wild: Now we must go home.

Jack: Yes! We can't wait to see Mel, Harry, Beth and Kit.

Why did Claudia want me and Toto? Because she liked us!

Why didn't we like Claudia? Because she was a robber!

① **Read the story and match.**

1 Why aren't Claudia and Magnus in the hotel?
2 Why did Claudia want Toto?
3 Why did she want Oscar?
4 Why didn't they buy some animals?
5 Why did the policeman thank Kelly and Jack?

a Because they were brave and helpful.
b Because they are going to go to prison.
c Because they are robbers.
d Because she collects rare birds.
e Because she liked him.

② **Choose and write.**

paintings   valuable   ~~robbers~~   diamonds   jewellery   stealing

This is Magnus and Claudia's house. Why did the police in Switzerland go there? Because they knew Claudia and Magnus were dangerous **(1)** _robbers_ !
They found many **(2)** .... things there.
Under the bed there was a big bag of **(3)** ....
In the cupboard there was a lot of **(4)** ....
and there were two **(5)** .... in front of
the bed. They liked **(6)** .... !

③ **Think and write with Dr Wild.**

Think about your favourite hobby. Tick the things you like about it and write.

I like swimming because I'm good at it and I like sport.

....
....
....
....

I can do it with my friends. ......
I can do it at home. ......
I can do it on my own. ......
I can do it at the weekends. ......

I like sport. ......
I like collecting things. ......
I'm happy when I'm doing it. ......
It's good fun. ......

I get lots of fresh air. ......
I wear special clothes. ......
I'm good at it. ......
I learn lots of new things. ......

WOULD YOU LIKE TO COME TO OUR PARTY?

To Roz

The occasion: A Welcome Home picnic for Jack and Kelly

The time: 3.00 in the afternoon

The date: Saturday August 8th

The place: Greenwoods Park

RSVP Tel: Kit 7855021   Email: kit@flyhigh.com

I've got an invitation from Kit!

1 Read and answer.

1 What is the occasion?

A Welcome Home picnic for Jack and Kelly

2 Where is the party?

....

3 What time is it?

....

4 Is Roz going to go?

....

5 Is she going to take anything to the picnic?

....

To: Kit@flyhigh.com

From: Roz@flyhigh.com

Subject: Party Invitation!

Dear Kit,

Thank you for the invitation to the Welcome Home picnic for Jack and Kelly. I'd love to come. I can't wait to see them and hear all their news. The last time I saw them was on May 22nd and it's August 3rd now! Would you like me to bring some food and drink to the picnic? I'll bring some sandwiches, crisps and juice.

Love, Roz

Writing Class: writing dates

2 Look at the example.

Then look at the invitation and message again and circle the dates.

Then write them in order.

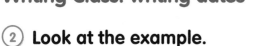

May 22nd

③ **Listen and circle.**

	1	**2**	**3**
Occasion	~~Birthday party~~ Fancy dress party	Birthday party Fancy dress party	Picnic School dance
Date	Saturday September 15th Saturday September 5th	Friday October 31st Friday October 3rd	Wednesday March 5th Wednesday March 25th
Time	7.30 5.30	3.45 4.15	7.30 5.30
Place	Peter's house The park	The school Tom's house	The school Kate's house

④ **Choose a party from 3 and complete.**

WOULD YOU LIKE TO COME TO MY
PARTY?

To ....

The
occasion: ....
....

The time: ....

The date: ....

The place: ....

RSVP Tel: ....   Email: ....

⑤ **Write. Then act it out.**

Would you like to come to .... ?

It's on ....

It's at ....

It's at ....

Bye!

Thank you. Yes, I'd love to come. When is it?

What time is it?

Where is it?

Great. See you then. Bye!

FlyHigh File: Duke of Edinburgh's Award

1 Read and number the photos.

Children of fourteen and over can do the Duke of Edinburgh's Award. A teacher helps them. It takes about six months to do an award.

You have to do something from each of these sections:

1 **Physical:** getting better at a sport or dancing

2 **Volunteering:** helping other people or animals

3 **Skills:** learning how to do something new

4 **Expedition:** going on a two-day trip and staying one night in a tent

② Read and write the sections from 1.

Planning for a Bronze medal

......Volunteering:....: You can help old people, children, people with special needs, animals or people who live on the streets. You can help with gardening, shopping, cooking, cleaning or talking to people who don't have friends or family. You must do volunteering for three months.

........................: What are your hobbies? You can do photography, computer skills, painting, singing, playing a musical instrument, sewing, knitting, making things or being a DJ! It doesn't matter what you do, the most important thing is to learn something new. You do this section for three months.

........................: What sport do you like doing? Choose your favourite and do something new in it for three months. You can do swimming, football, basketball, climbing, tennis or dancing. You can do anything! The idea is to get fitter and better at it.

........................: You do this with four to seven other people. You can go sailing, walking, cycling, horse riding or climbing. You plan the two-day expedition; what you're going to eat and where you're going to go, and you camp for one night in a tent. It's a great adventure!

③ Read and complete.

Sections	Volunteering	Physical	Expedition	Skills
Three things you can do	1 helping children 2 .... 3	1 .... 2 .... 3	1 .... 2 .... 3	1 .... 2 .... 3 ....
How long does it take?	3 months	....	....	....

My Project

Complete the plan for you and write.

	do a sport	help people	learn something new
What are you going to do?	football	shopping for grandma	
When are you going to start?	Monday	tomorrow	

I'm going to do two things.

I'm going to learn to play football better.

I'm going to start on Monday.

I'm going to help people too.

I'm going to do the shopping for my grandma.

I'm going to start tomorrow!

The FlyHigh Review

1 **Say it with Aunt Sophie.**

a) Listen and point. Then repeat.

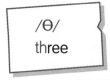 /θ/ three

 /t/ tree

 /f/ free

 /tʃ/ cheap

b) Listen and circle. Then say all the words.

1	(three)	tree	**6**	teach	teeth
2	fair	their	**7**	fat	that
3	month	munch	**8**	thank	tank
4	eight	eighth	**9**	teas	these
5	thin	fin			

2 **What about you? Complete and write your answers.**

cycling   tobogganing   ~~ice skating~~   rock climbing   fishing   skateboarding

1 Do you like ___ice skating?___ ?
Yes, I do / No, I don't .

2 Are you good at ___ ?
___ .

3 Do you want to go ___ ?
___ .

4 Are you happy when you are ___ ?
___ .

5 Do you like ___ ?
___ .

6 Do you want to go ___ ?
___ .

3 **Listen and match. Then ask and answer.**

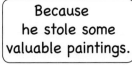

Why is this robber in prison?

Because he stole some valuable paintings.

④ **Look, circle and write.**

knock over ~~jump on~~ close sit on clean use
~~the sofa~~ the cushion the phone the rug the lamp the curtains

1 The cat (is) / are going to ___jump on the sofa___ .

2 Grandpa is / are going to _____ .

3 The girl is / are going to _____ .

4 The boy and the dog is / are going to
_____ .

5 Mum is / are going to _____ .

6 Dad is / are going to _____ .

⑤ **Write the correct form of want to and match.**

1 ☺ We _____want to_____ to borrow   the team.

2 ☹ He _____ join   a gold medal.

3 ☺ I _____ be   a basketball.

4 ☹ They _____ us to score   a good swimmer.

5 ☺ She _____ win   a goal.

⑥ **Write.**

1 What shall we __do_____ (do) on
Saturday?

What about __having____ (have)
a picnic?

2 Where shall we _____ (go) ?

What about _____ (go) to
the park?

3 What about _____ (send)
invitations?

Shall we _____ (invite)
everybody?

4 What shall we _____ (wear) ?

What about _____ (wear)
fancy dress costumes?

The Voyages of Sindbad the Sailor

1 Read and listen.

PENGUIN READERS

The Voyages of
Sindbad the Sailor

I am Sindbad the **Sailor**. This is the story of my sixth **voyage**. 'I will make one last voyage,' I thought.

It was a long and **dangerous** voyage. It was very windy. We were lost. The **captain** pointed to a mountain in front of us.

'Can you see that mountain?' the captain shouted. 'There is a cave at its foot. The sea will take our **ship** into it. I cannot stop it now. There is no way out of the cave. When a man goes in there, he dies!'

The sailors tried to **sail** the ship out of the fast water but they could do nothing. The mountain came nearer and nearer. Suddenly the water carried our ship into the cave. Inside, the ship hit the walls and broke. There were men and **wood** everywhere in the water.

'Where are you?' I called.

I listened but nobody answered. I could do nothing to help my friends. The water was fast and it carried me through the cave on some wood from the ship.

My journey through those black caves was very long. I was tired and **afraid**. I fell asleep.

I woke to the sound of shouts. I opened my eyes and looked around me. I was next to a great river. People looked down on me. The noise came from them.

'Who are you?' I asked. 'Can you help me?'

They answered me, 'You are in the country of the great king of Serendip.'

I was happy then because I knew about this great king and his country. I knew he was kind to people.

'These mountains are dangerous. How did you come here?'

'I will tell you my story,' I said.

I told them how our ship went into the cave near the sea and broke on the walls.

I cried. 'My friends are dead. I was afraid on that long and dangerous journey!'

A man said 'You must tell this story to the king. We will take you to him now.'

They brought a horse for me and we left the river. After three days we arrived at the king's city and the men went to see him.

The king liked the story of my great adventure. He wanted to hear more stories. He was kind. He gave me rooms and the best clothes and food and other good things. He sent for me day after day and I told him the story of all my voyages.

One day I heard about a ship.

'This ship is going to my city,' I said. 'Can I go home now?'

'Yes, go,' said the king. 'I will give you a letter for your king and many rich things for you and him.'

'Thank you,' I answered. The king sent many beautiful things from Serendip.

I had a good voyage home and I took the presents to the king. Then I went back to my house and met my friends again.

Glossary

afraid	this means 'scared'
....	the person in command of a ship
....	something that can hurt or kill you is this
....	travel in a ship or boat
....	someone who works on a boat or ship
....	a big boat
....	a long trip by sea
....	trees are made of this

33

 disappear
 explain
 return
 hot air balloon
 trip

Jack has disappeared!

1. Where's Jack?

I don't know. We've rescued Oscar and Toto and now Jack has disappeared.

2. I've looked everywhere and I can't find him.

This is Mr Falcon. I've explained that we need to return home. He's got a hot air balloon we can use.

3. Here he is.

There's somebody with him.

That's wonderful. I've flown a balloon lots of times before.

5. Off we go.

6. Look at the fields and that big forest over there.

7. Hooray! We're home.

We've really enjoyed this trip. Thank you, Aunt Sophie.

We've rescued Oscar. He's jumped into the hot air balloon.

Learn with Oscar

I/You/We/They	He/She/It
They have returned home.	He has returned home.
have = 've	has = 's

① **Read the story and number in order.**

☐ **a** Dr Wild has noticed a forest.

☐ **b** Jack has returned with a man.

☐ **c** They've arrived home from the trip.

1 **d** Jack has disappeared.

☐ **e** Jack has explained that they need to go home.

☐ **f** Kelly has looked everywhere for Jack.

② **Listen and circle the correct pictures. Then say.**

wash

clean

paint

start

She's washed the curtain.

③ **Circle, choose and write.**

open ~~return~~ email watch talk jump

It's half past six now.

1 They 's /(ve) returned home safely.

2 Kelly 's / 've .... the invitation to the picnic.

3 Jack 's / 've .... some photos to Harry.

4 Dr Wild 's / 've .... to Sally on the phone.

5 Oscar 's / 've .... on the sofa.

6 They 's / 've .... the News.

34

 horse riding

 camping

 canoeing

 Chinese

 restaurant

Have you seen these photos?

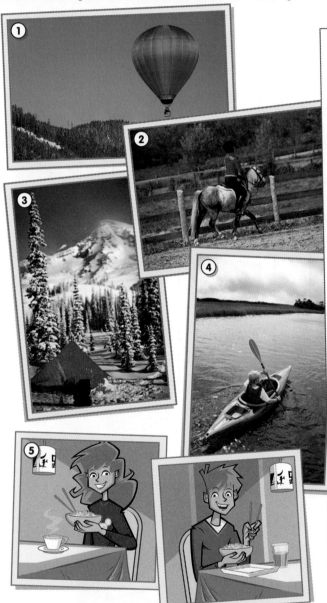

Kit: Wow! Have you seen these photos? Jack has sent us some photos of their trip. Here they are in a hot air balloon. Have you ever flown in a hot air balloon?

Beth: No, I haven't but I've been in a plane. We went to America last year. Have you been to America?

Kit: No, I haven't.

Beth: Here's Kelly at that farm. She's riding a horse. I love horse riding.

Kit: I've never ridden a horse.

Beth: I don't know when they took this photo. It's a tent in the mountains.

Kit: Perhaps they went camping.

Beth: I've never slept in a tent.

Kit: I have. We go camping every summer. It's great.

Kit: Look at this photo. Jack is canoeing.

Beth: Have you ever been canoeing?

Kit: Yes, I have. It was great.

Beth: Here they are in a Chinese restaurant. Have you ever eaten Chinese food?

Kit: Yes, I have. It was delicious.

① Read and answer.

1 Beth has flown in   **a)** a plane.   **b)** a hot air balloon.
2 Beth has been to   **a)** Russia.   **b)** America.
3 Beth has ridden   **a)** an elephant.   **b)** a horse.
4 Kit has slept   **a)** in a tent.   **b)** on a farm.
5 Kit has been   **a)** horse riding.   **b)** canoeing.
6 Kit has eaten   **a)** Chinese food.   **b)** American food.

Have you ever flown in a hot air balloon?
Yes, I have.

see	seen
send	sent
fly	flown
be/go	been
eat	eaten
sleep	slept
ride	ridden

Has Kit ever been to America?
No, he hasn't. He hasn't been to America.

---

② **Complete with a tick or cross. Then ask and answer.**

ridden a horse/been canoeing/flown in a plane/seen a hot air balloon/eaten Chinese food/slept in a tent

You						
Your friend						

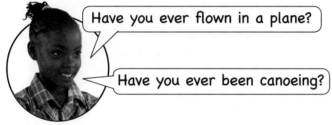

Have you ever flown in a plane?

Have you ever been canoeing?

Yes, I have.

No, I haven't.

③ **Write.**

1 I have ....   3 My friend has ....

2 I haven't ....   4 My friend hasn't ....

④ **Sing. Then ask and answer the questions.**

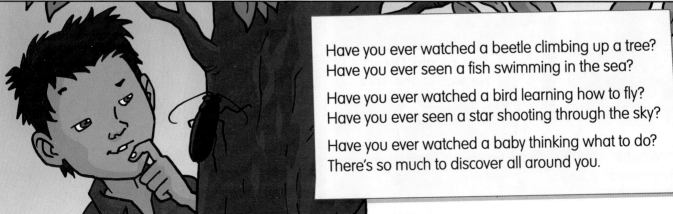

Have you ever watched a beetle climbing up a tree?
Have you ever seen a fish swimming in the sea?

Have you ever watched a bird learning how to fly?
Have you ever seen a star shooting through the sky?

Have you ever watched a baby thinking what to do?
There's so much to discover all around you.

 brush polish change

I haven't brushed Oscar yet!

1 Kelly, are you ready for the picnic?

Yes, I am. I've polished my shoes and I've changed into my new dress.

2 Have you changed yet, Jack?

No, I haven't. I can't find my new T-shirt.

It's on your bed!

3 I haven't brushed Oscar yet. Has anybody seen him?

Yes, I have. Look. He's hiding. He doesn't like the brush.

4 Have you caught Oscar yet?

No we haven't. He's gone into the garden now.

5 Help!

I've caught Oscar! He was in the tree.

What's happened?

6 Oh no!

Bad luck, Kelly. You need to change again!

Learn with Oscar

have	had
catch	caught
go	gone
give	given

① **Read the story and tick the correct sentence.**

Picture 1 a) Kelly has polished her shoes.　✔......

　　　　　b) Kelly hasn't polished her shoes yet.　......

Picture 2 a) Jack has changed his clothes.　......

　　　　　b) Jack hasn't changed his clothes yet.　......

Picture 3 a) Dr Wild has brushed Oscar.　......

　　　　　b) Dr Wild hasn't brushed Oscar yet.　......

Picture 4 a) They have caught Oscar.　......

　　　　　b) They haven't caught Oscar yet.　......

Picture 5 a) Kelly has caught Oscar.　......

　　　　　b) Kelly hasn't caught Oscar yet.　......

② **Look and tick or cross. Then ask and answer.**

It's twenty to three.
The picnic is at three o'clock.

1　washed her hands and face　✔......

2　brushed her hair　......

3　changed her clothes　......

4　polished her shoes　......

5　put her coat on　......

> Has Kelly washed her hands and face yet?

> Yes, she has.

③ **Think and write with Dr Wild.**

had a shower
brushed your hair
eaten your breakfast
learnt some English
had lunch
done your homework
talked to your friends
tidied your room
watched TV

> Write what you have done today and what you haven't done yet.

I've eaten my breakfast.
I haven't had lunch yet.
....
....
....
....

You should take your camera.

36 SKILLS

1 **Read and tick the animals Sally has seen.**

Dear Kelly and Jack

Thank you very much for rescuing Toto. Your aunt has told me how helpful you were. We're very happy that he's back at the zoo. He's very happy too! I've come to South Africa for a holiday. Have you ever been to South Africa? It's a beautiful country and I've seen a lot of amazing animals here — hippos, zebras, giraffes, elephants, lions and a rhino. They live in the wild in Kruger National Park. Tomorrow is my last day and I want to go on a trip in a hot air balloon. I hope I don't fall out! See you back in England.

Love from Sally

Miss K and Mr J Wild

8 Tower Street

Bristol, BR8 1JP

2 **Read and answer.**

1 Who has talked to Sally?

2 Where is Toto?

3 Where is Sally?

4 Do the giraffes live in the zoo?

5 What does Sally want to do tomorrow?

Writing Class: writing an address

3 **Look at the example.**

Find the address and answer the questions.

House number, street name: 17 Castle Road
Town or city: London
Postcode: E12 7RJ

1 Who is the postcard to?

....

2 What house number and street do they live in?

....

3 What town do they live in?

....

4 What is the postcode?

....

4 Listen and match.

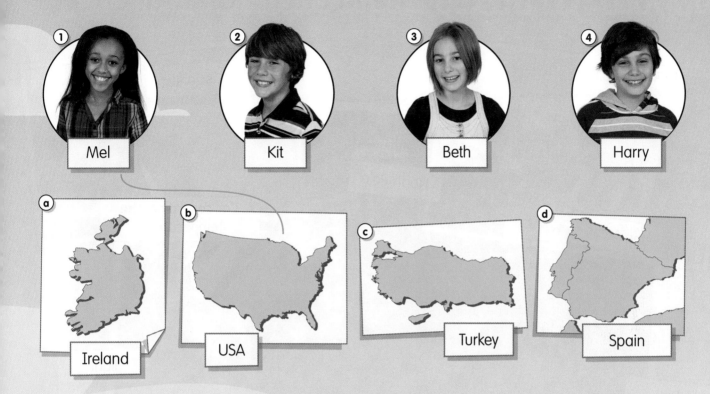

1 Mel
2 Kit
3 Beth
4 Harry

a Ireland
b USA
c Turkey
d Spain

5 Listen again and complete the chart.

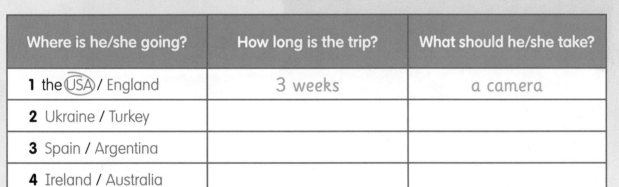

Where is he/she going?	How long is the trip?	What should he/she take?
1 the USA / England	3 weeks	a camera
2 Ukraine / Turkey		
3 Spain / Argentina		
4 Ireland / Australia		

6 Choose from the ideas in 5 and write. Then act it out.

I'm so excited. We're going to .... tomorrow.

Have you been there before?

No, I haven't. It's my first visit.

How long are you going for?

....

That's a good idea. Thank you.

It's [ ] [ ] [ ] You should take ....

FlyHigh File: The Arctic and Antarctic

the Arctic

North Pole

scientist

I'm recording the temperature.

dark

light

South Pole

the Antarctic

① **Guess and tick or cross.**

	polar bear	walrus	seal	fox	whale	penguin
The Arctic	✔					
The Antarctic	✘					

2 Read and check.

The Arctic and Antarctic are the coldest places on Earth. There's a lot of snow and ice and it's always cold. In summer it's light all day and all night. In winter it's dark all the time.

The Arctic is an exciting place full of animals, birds and people. There are small towns with shops, cafés, libraries and schools. Whales, walruses, seals, foxes and polar bears live near the North Pole. In winter many animals, such as foxes and birds, change colour. They change from brown to white so they can hide in the snow from other animals.

In the Antarctic there are no trees or flowers because it's too cold. It's colder than the Arctic, and on 21st July 1983 the temperature was minus 89°C. This is the lowest temperature ever recorded. It's the coldest, windiest and driest continent on the planet. The Antarctic has about 90% of the world's ice.

There are very few people in the Antarctic – only a few scientists visiting the Research Stations. However, you can travel there for a holiday. People go to the Antarctic because it's very beautiful and there are a lot of birds and animals to see. There aren't any polar bears, foxes or walruses but there are whales and seals and seventeen different kinds of penguin. It's an amazing place.

3 Read and write Arctic or Antarctic.

1 The South Pole is in the middle of this continent.
Antarctic

2 It's the windiest place in the world.

3 Animals change colour in winter.

4 Penguins live here.

5 You can see polar bears and walruses here.

6 It has the coldest temperature ever recorded.

7 People live here.

8 Scientists visit here to do research.

My Project

Design and make a poster about your country for a visitor.

Ireland is a small island. There are a lot of hills and rivers in Ireland. It's very green because it rains a lot. You can see a lot of birds and farm animals. There are cows, sheep and horses in the fields. It's very pretty.

Goodbye

Party time!

① **Listen and read. Then ask and answer.**

What was your favourite part of the story?

I liked ....

(2) **Sing.**

We've learnt lots of new things,
And made some new friends too.
We've had parties and meals and trips,
There were so many things to do!

What a great adventure!
What a lot of fun!
We've had good times, happy times, funny times,
Now our work is done!

We've all been together,
In good times and in bad.
We've laughed and sung and worked and played,
What a good time we've had!

What a great adventure!
What a lot of fun!
We've had good times, happy times, funny times,
Now our work is done!

The FlyHigh Review

① **Say it with Aunt Sophie.** 💿

a) Listen and point. Then repeat.

/ɑː/ car	/eə/ care	/ɜː/ her	/ɪə/ here

/ɪ/ kit	/aɪ/ kite

b) Listen and write the correct letters. Then repeat.

1 pl _a_ n   pl _a_ ne
2 b ___ t   b ___ te
3 m ___ d   m ___ de
4 ___ s   ___ se
5 h ___ p   h ___ pe
6 f ___ n   f ___ ne

7 f ___ r   f ___ re
8 ___ t   ___ te
9 p ___ n   p ___ ne
10 r ___ d   r ___ de
11 n ___ t   n ___ te
12 b ___ r   b ___ re

② **Complete and number.**

a  ☐

b  ☐

c  1

d  ☐

e ☐

f  ☐

1 The children _have arrived_ (arrive) at the theatre.

2 The race .... (not start) yet.

3 They .... (not watch) the DVD yet.

4 The teacher .... (explain) where polar bears live.

5 The class .... (return) from the school trip.

6 The Art lesson .... (not finish) yet.

③ **Write questions and answers.**

1 (see) _Has he ever seen_ a hippo?   _Yes, he has._

2 (ride) _Has he ever ridden_ a horse?   _No, he hasn't._

3 (catch) .... a fish?   ....

4 (eat) .... carrot cake?   ....

5 (be) .... the USA?   ....

6 (sleep) .... in a tent?   ....

④ **Look and write should and the correct verb.**

polish   change   wash   ~~brush~~   have

① ② ③ ④ ⑤

1 Her hair is a mess. She ....should brush.... it.

2 It's lunchtime. She .... her hands.

3 She's going to a party. She .... her clothes.

4 Her shoes are dirty. She .... them.

5 It's bedtime. She .... a shower.

⑤ **Listen and tick or cross. Then write about their holiday plans.**

① Mel   ② Beth   ③ Harry and Kit

1 Mel ...isn't going to... go cycling.

She ...'s going to... play tennis.

2 Beth .... go canoeing.

She .... go sailing.

3 Harry and Kit .... go camping.

They .... go horse riding.

⑥ **What about you? Write about your holiday plans.**

1 Where are you going to go on holiday? ....

2 How are you going to get there? ....

3 Who are you going to go with? ....

4 Where are you going to stay? ....

5 What are you going to do? ....

6 Are you going to go swimming? ....

The FlyHigh Show

The amazing adventure!

Child 1: What shall we do today?

Child 2: I don't know. What's the weather like?

Child 3: It's raining.

Child 4: Do we have to do our homework?

All: No! It's Saturday!

All sing: What do you have to do today? (Lesson 18)

Child 5: There are big black clouds in the sky and it's raining a lot now!

Child 6: It's very windy too.

Child 1: I like storms!

Child 2: What did you do yesterday? Did you do anything exciting?

All sing: Did you have a good day yesterday? (Lesson 10)

Child 3: Well, we had a good day yesterday.

Child 4: But it wasn't very exciting.

Child 5: We went to school.

Child 6: I helped my parents.

All sing: Yesterday I stayed at home. (Lesson 6)

Child 1: I played with my old toys. Look. This is my old train. I loved this when I was younger. It was my favourite toy.

Child 2: Look! Can you see what I can see?

Child 3: It's a train!

Child 4: Where did it come from?

Child 5: It came with the storm!

Child 6: Look. There's a train driver. She's coming here.

Train driver: Come with me. We're going on an adventure!

Child 4: It's stopped raining now!

Child 5: Where are we going?

Girl train driver: It's a surprise. Follow me!

Child 1: Do we need tickets?

Girl train driver: Don't worry. I've got them!

All sing: We're travelling on the train. (Lesson 14)

Girl train driver: The train has stopped. We've arrived.

Child 2: Where are we?

Child 3: I can see the sea and some animals.

Child 4: Are they cows or horses?

Child 5: No, I think they're …

All children: Dinosaurs!

Child 6: We're in the past!

Girl train driver: Don't be scared. We can see the dinosaurs but they can't see us.

Child 1: The world looks different.

Child 2: Yes, it does. Some of the dinosaurs are flying, some are swimming.

Child 3: Take a photo.

Child 4: I haven't got my camera!

Child 5: This is amazing.

Girl train driver: Yes. Planet Earth is amazing and full of surprises!

All sing: Have you ever watched a beetle climbing up a tree? (Lesson 34)

Girl train driver: Time to go home!

Child 1: Can we stay here a bit longer?

Girl train driver: I'm afraid not. Your parents will be worried. Everybody back on the train.

All children: Goodbye dinosaurs.

[Train driver exits quietly while the other children are not looking]

Child 2: Home again.

Child 3: Thank you. That was a wonderful adventure.

Child 4: Where's the train driver?

Child 5: She's gone!

Child 6: Did that really happen? Did we really go on a train and see dinosaurs?

Child 1: I don't know. I'm confused!

Child 2: But we had great fun.

All children: Yes, we did!

All sing: We've learnt lots of new things. (Goodbye)

Teacher's Day

 Ancient Greece wax stick wrestling strict hit

What is your teacher called? Is your teacher a man or a woman? How many teachers are there in your school?

In Ancient Greece the teachers were all men. There weren't any women teachers. There were grammar teachers, music teachers and PE teachers.

They didn't have blackboards or books. They wrote lessons for the children on wood. There was wax on the wood. They didn't have pens, they had sticks. They taught reading, writing, thinking and music. In the afternoons the PE teachers taught wrestling!

Much later, in the eighteenth century, there were women and men teachers. The teachers were very strict then and they sometimes hit the children with sticks.

In the nineteenth century the famous English author Charles Dickens wrote about a very strict teacher in his book

Hard Times. The teacher's name was Mr Gradgrind. He didn't like children thinking and having ideas. He said they must only learn facts. Teachers wrote on blackboards at the front of the class.

Today there are books, pens and computers and games in our schools. Men and women can be teachers. In their classrooms they sometimes have blackboards like in the 1800s but now they have whiteboards as well. Our teachers are sometimes strict but they are kind too and they like children thinking and having lots of ideas!

① Read and write True or False.

1 There were men and women teachers in Ancient Greece. ....

2 Teachers wrote on blackboards in Ancient Greece. ....

3 PE teachers taught wrestling in the afternoons in Ancient Greece. ....

4 Charles Dickens was a famous English writer. ....

5 Mr Gradgrind was a kind teacher. ....

6 In the 18th century the teachers sometimes hit the children. ....

② **Listen and circle.** 💿

1 Mrs Baker teaches   **a** (English.)   **b** Maths.   **c** Science.

2 Her favourite food is   **a** chicken sandwiches.   **b** chicken and salad.   **c** chicken and chips.

3 She would like to go to   **a** England.   **b** Russia.   **c** India.

4 She's got a   **a** white cat.   **b** big cat.   **c** white dog.

5 Her favourite sport is   **a** football.   **b** walking.   **c** swimming.

6 Her favourite clothes are   **a** red skirt / black sweater.   **b** red sweater / black skirt.   **c** red dress / black shoes.

③ **What do you know about your teacher? Guess, then ask and write.**

	My guess	My teacher's answer
What's your favourite food?		
Where in the world do you want to go?		
Have you got any pets?		
What's your favourite sport?		
What are your favourite clothes?		

What's your favourite food?

Cheese sandwiches.

④ **Listen and number. Then sing.** 💿

.... You teach us what is wrong and right,

.... And lots of games to play.

.... You teach us words to say.

_1_ You teach us how to think and write,

.... And we have lots of fun as well,

.... Teacher, we love you!

.... You teach us how to read and spell,

.... You teach us what to do.

Valentine's Day

 message   rose   violet   heart

1 Guess and circle. Then read and check.

1 When is Valentine's Day?	February 14th / May 1st / July 4th
2 How old is Valentine's Day?	100 years old / 300 years old / 600 years old
3 What do people send on Valentine's Day?	money / cards / clothes
4 What do people give on Valentine's Day?	eggs / birds / flowers

February 14th is a special day. It's Valentine's Day. It's a day to tell somebody that you love them. This tradition started in Europe more than 600 years ago. About 200 years ago, people started sending Valentine's cards. The cards have messages of friendship and love. Sometimes the cards do not say who they are from. It's a secret and the person never knows who sent the card. Today people send cards or give presents, such as flowers and chocolates, on Valentine's Day.

2 Listen to the traditional Valentine's messages and circle.

1
(1) Roses / Tomatoes are red
(2) Oceans / Violets are blue
(3) Sugar / Honey is sweet
And so are you.

2
My love is like a (4) carrot / cabbage
Cut up into (5) two / three
The (6) leaves / flowers I give to others
The (7) eyes / heart I give to you.

3 **Read and tick the Valentine's Day messages.**

My best friend is the one who brings out the best in me.

I love you. Be my Valentine. xxx

Happy Easter

I GIVE YOU MY HEART. BE MINE.

Happy Birthday to you

HAPPY VALENTINE'S DAY

Merry Christmas

4 **Choose a message and make a Valentine card for your friend.**

Happy valentine's Day

I love you

5 **Read and learn the poem.**

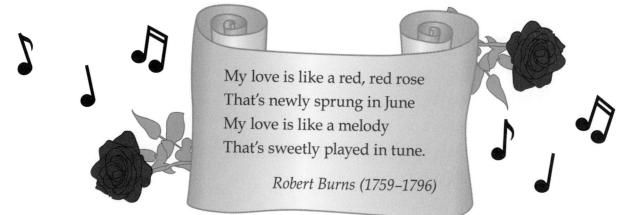

My love is like a red, red rose
That's newly sprung in June
My love is like a melody
That's sweetly played in tune.

Robert Burns (1759–1796)

The Queen's Birthday

gun salute

garden

midday

parade

1 The Queen

The kings and queens of the United Kingdom celebrate two birthdays every year. Queen Elizabeth II was born on April 21st 1926. This is her real birthday. She also has an official birthday on a Saturday in June.

On April 21st the Queen spends a quiet day with her family and friends. At midday there are gun salutes in London – a 41-gun salute in Hyde Park, a 21-gun salute

2 A 21-gun salute

in Windsor Great Park and a 62-gun salute in the Tower of London. On special birthdays the National Anthem is played on the radio. There aren't any big celebrations in April.

The main celebrations are in June, because the weather is usually better than in April. On her official birthday the Queen and her family watch

3 The Trooping of the Colour

soldiers in a parade called the Trooping of the Colour. Thousands of people from around the world watch the Birthday Parade with her. This tradition started in 1748. It's the biggest royal celebration of the year in Britain.

② Read and complete.

1 The Queen was born in ....April............. .

2 The Queen's official birthday is in ....

3 On the Queen's real birthday there are gun salutes in ....

4 The Trooping of the Colour for the King or Queen's birthday started in ....

5 The Birthday Parade is the biggest ....

2 Listen and circle.

1 It's June 12th / June 14th.
2 At twenty to eleven the Queen leaves
   the Tower of London / Buckingham Palace.
3 The parade starts at
   eleven o'clock / half past eleven.
4 The foot soldiers and the soldiers on horses follow
   the Queen / the bands.
5 The parade lasts about an hour / two hours.
6 The planes fly past Buckingham Palace at
   half past twelve / one o'clock.

3 Listen to the British National Anthem and number the lines in order.

..... Long to reign over us

..... God save the Queen.

..... Long live our noble Queen!

..... Happy and glorious,

..1.. God save our gracious Queen!

..... Send her victorious,

..... God save the Queen.

4 Choose and make an official birthday programme. Then ask and answer.

When is your official birthday?
....

What kind of celebration are you going to have?
....

Where is it going to be?
....

Who are you going to invite?
....

What are you going to do?
....

My official birthday is on December 1st.

On my birthday I want to have a snow party in the forest.

I'm going to invite my friends.

We're going to make a snowman.

Then we're going to go for a ride on a dog sled.

Afterwards we're going to cook sausages in a tent.

Word List

Welcome: A great adventure!

detective
missing

1 Where's Toto?

clever
niece
nephew
friendly
helpful

2 We're getting ready!

laptop
binoculars
compass
can opener
need
diary
torch

3 Dr Wild drives well.

well
carefully
badly
slowly
quietly
happily
quickly

Fly High File: Countries and nationalities

country
capital city
flag
nationality
language

5 There was a storm.

storm
behind
windy
thunder and lightning
in front of

6 We landed on a beach.

aquarium
town hall
police station
pet shop
museum
café

7 Did you talk to them?

notice
blond
moustache
beard
thin
wavy
face

Fly High File: Hurricanes

hurricane
last
flood
cause
tornado
produce
travel
destroy
natural disaster

Storytime: Robinson Crusoe

ill
tool
gun
knife
journey
land
island
tent
cave
strange
footprint

9 Magnus and Claudia had an accident!

farm
cow
grass
owl
pond
bull

10 Did they find Toto?

scared
confused
nervous
unhappy

11 Claudia couldn't hear.

well
cold
headache
sore throat
earache
ill
stomachache

Fly High File: Dinosaurs

continent
plant
lizard
land
sea
sky

13 They went through the town.

train station
road
market
castle
bridge

14 How much were the tickets?

money
seat
search
carriage
look after
luggage

15 I heard something!

stew
rice
cabbage
steak
peas

Fly High File: London bus tour

art gallery
church
cathedral
tower
Big Wheel
bell
hill
street

Storytime: Alice in Wonderland

hare
place
wine
tea
polite
wide
angrily

17 Is it yours?

rescue
scarf
glove
jacket
belt
trainers
tie

18 You don't have to shout!

arrive
leave
start
lose
bring
finish

19 Dr Wild went to the bank to get some money.

bank
post office
send
find
garage
hire

Fly High File: Clothes through the ages

eleventh – 11th
twelfth – 12th
thirteenth – 13th
fourteenth – 14th
fifteenth – 15th
sixteenth – 16th
seventeenth – 17th
eighteenth – 18th
nineteenth – 19th
twentieth – 20th
twenty-first – 21st
breeches
cap
trainers
tunic
apron

21 The red van is faster!

van
motorbike
fire engine
scooter
helicopter

22 They are the silliest people in the world!

silly
catch
runner
noisy
light

23 Oscar's got the most comfortable bed!

expensive
soft
comfortable
modern
dangerous
exciting
tobogganing

Fly High File: Planets

planet
rock
ring
gas
star
ice
furthest

Storytime: The Prince and the Pauper

palace
poor
beg
gates
soldiers
beggar
rich
servant
cheap
pauper

25 I want to join in.

join in
fancy dress
costume
alien
superhero
pop star

26 He likes tobogganing!
ice skating
surfing
skateboarding
rock climbing
cycling
fishing

27 What shall we do?
use
escape
reach
borrow
hold

Fly High File: Sporting legends
football player
score
goal
world record
Olympic flag
gold medal
medicine
compete
train

29 I'm going to phone the police!
knock over
lamp
curtain
rug
sofa
cushion
prison

30 Are they going to come home now?
plan
picnic
invitation
banner

31 Why did they want Toto?
rare
robber
steal
jewellery
valuable
painting
diamond

Fly High File: Duke of Edinburgh's Award
award
physical
volunteering
skills
expedition
photography
sewing
knitting
DJ

Storytime: The Voyages of Sindbad the Sailor
sailor
voyage
dangerous
captain
ship
sail
wood
afraid

33 Jack has disappeared!
disappear
explain
return
hot air balloon
trip

34 Have you seen these photos?
horse riding
camping
canoeing
Chinese
restaurant

35 I haven't brushed Oscar yet!
brush
polish
change

Fly High File: The Arctic and Antarctic
North Pole
South Pole
Arctic
Antarctic
scientist
light
dark
polar bear
walrus
seal
fox

Teacher's Day
Ancient Greece
wax
stick
wrestling
strict
hit

Valentine's Day
message
rose
violet
heart

The Queen's Birthday
gun salute
garden
midday
parade

Irregular Verbs

Base Form	Simple Past	Past Participle	Base Form	Simple Past	Past Participle
be	was/were	been	lose	lost	lost
begin	began	begun	make	made	made
bring	brought	brought	meet	met	met
buy	bought	bought	put	put	put
catch	caught	caught	read	read	read
come	came	come	ride	rode	ridden
cut	cut	cut	ring	rang	rung
do	did	done	run	ran	run
draw	drew	drawn	say	said	said
drink	drank	drunk	see	saw	seen
drive	drove	driven	sell	sold	sold
eat	ate	eaten	send	sent	sent
fall	fell	fallen	sing	sang	sung
feed	fed	fed	sit	sat	satwa
feel	felt	felt	sleep	slept	slept
fight	fought	fought	speak	spoke	spoken
find	found	found	stand	stood	stood
fly	flew	flown	steal	stole	stolen
get	got	got	swim	swam	swum
give	gave	given	take	took	taken
go	went	gone	tell	told	told
grow	grew	grown	think	thought	thought
hear	heard	heard	throw	threw	thrown
hide	hid	hidden	understand	understood	understood
hit	hit	hit	wake up	woke up	woken up
hold	held	held	wear	wore	worn
know	knew	known	write	wrote	written
learn	learnt	learnt			
leave	left	left			

First published 2011
Sixteenth impression 2020

ISBN: 978-1-4082-4823-2

Printed in Italy by L.E.G.O. S.p.A.

Set in VagRounded

Acknowledgements
Alamy Images: ACE STOCK LIMITED 80bl, Alan Keith Beastall 80tl, amana images inc. 120, Anthony Kay / Flight 14tr, Ben Molyneux Travel Photography 46b, chrisstockphoto 80tr, Colin Palmer Photography 46cr, CountrySideCollection - Homer Sykes 96bl, imagebroker 17br, 22t, Johannes Leber 104t, Kuttig - People 48b, mediablitzimages (uk) Limited 84c, Neil McAllister 49r, OJO Images Ltd 14br, Paul Springett A 108bc, PhotoAlto 14cl, Rob Walls 96tr, SHOUT 60bl; **Jon Barlow:** 8, 9, 12, 15, 18, 22c, 22b, 23t, 25, 32, 42, 46tr, 56, 61t, 66, 70, 71t, 79l, 81t, 84, 90, 94, 109t, 112-113t, 121; **Trevor Clifford:** 13, 17c, 19, 21, 23c, 23b, 37, 47, 51, 57, 61b, 62, 65, 67, 71b, 79br, 81b, 85, 89, 91, 95, 98, 103, 105, 109b, 112b, 119l; **Corbis:** Radius Images 80br; **Education Photos:** John Walmsley 60t; Fotolia.com: allievn 108bl, Lance Bellers 46cl, Peter Betts 108 (lion); **Getty Images:** 122bl, Anwar Hussein 122r, Digital Vision / Inti St Clair 96br, Harry How 86bl, Joern Pollex 86tl, Jupiterimages 14cr, Kyle Niemi / US Coast Guard 24tr, Mike Theiss / National Geographic 24br, Pando Hall 123tr, Peter Cade 14bl, Peter Teller 96tl, Samir Hussein 123tl, Science Faction 104cl, Shaun Botterill 86tr, Sports Illustrated 87, Tim Graham 123c; **iStockphoto:** blackwaterimages 119r; **Pearson Education Ltd:** Digital Stock 108 (zebra), Digital Vision 108 (giraffe), Photodisc / Getty Images 24bl, Photodisc / Jack Hollingsworth Photography 108tl, Photodisc / StockTrek 24tl, Photodisc. Alan D. Carey 108br; **Reuters:** Wolfgang Rattay (CHINA) 86br; **Rex Features:** 122tl; **Shutterstock.com:** 46tl; **Thinkstock:** 49l, 60c, 60br, Football / 84cl, 104cr, Digital Vision 108 (hippo), Hemera 84bl, 104tr, 111r, Hemera Technologies 84cr, iStockphoto 84br, Medioimages / Photodisc 111l, Stockbyte 84b, 84bl (2)

All other images © Pearson Education

Every effort has been made to trace the copyright holders and we apologise in advance for any unintentional omissions. We would be pleased to insert the appropriate acknowledgement in any subsequent edition of this publication.

Illustrated by Diego Diaz/Lemonade Illustration; Sean Longcroft; Stephanie Strickland; Jurgen Ziewe/Debut Art; Vasili Zorin/Debut Art;